“It is no surprise that this luci
a fraught topic should come
Sonn, one of the leading scholars of Islam today. The author trenchantly analyses some of the most pervasive contemporary stereotypes of Muslims – especially their alleged proclivity for violence – and confronts lurid depictions of Islam with sober facts. The result is a highly accessible and valuable study that compellingly undermines the all-too-common view that ‘Islam’ and ‘the West’ are at war with one another.”

Asma Afsaruddin, Indiana University

“Tamara Sonn’s new book dispels the myths that portray Islam as inherently violent and antagonistic toward the West. She offers a compelling response and an essential antidote to the crude caricatures of Islam that pervade our post-9/11 world.”

Todd Green, Luther College and author of *The Fear of Islam: An Introduction to Islamophobia in the West*

“Sonn’s excellent analysis introduces the reader to the voices of mainstream Muslims who speak out against terrorism, voices that tend to be drowned in the public discourse. Sonn convincingly argues that common grievances among Muslims should not be confused with common religious beliefs. This incisive little book is a reminder that politics, and not religion, is the cause of grievances that lead some to engage in terrorism.”

Nelly Lahoud, Institute for Strategic Studies-Middle East

“A concise but remarkably comprehensive analysis of a major element in contemporary global affairs – the relations between Islam and the West. Sonn’s thorough knowledge of both mainstream and extremist Muslim thought and movements gives a depth to this study that goes well beyond the usual coverage of this significant subject.”

John O. Voll, Georgetown University

Is Islam an Enemy of the West?

Global Futures

Mohammed Ayoob, *Will the Middle East Implode?*
Christopher Coker, *Can War be Eliminated?*
Howard Davies, *Can Financial Markets be Controlled?*
Jonathan Fenby, *Will China Dominate the 21st Century?*
Andrew Gamble, *Can the Welfare State Survive?*
David Hulme, *Should Rich Nations Help the Poor?*
Joseph S. Nye Jr., *Is the American Century Over?*
Dmitri Trenin, *Should We Fear Russia?*
Jan Zielonka, *Is the EU Doomed?*

Tamara Sonn

Is Islam an Enemy of the West?

polity

First published in 2016 by Polity Press

Polity Press
65 Bridge Street
Cambridge CB2 1UR, UK

Polity Press
350 Main Street
Malden, MA 02148, USA

ISBN-13: 978-1-5095-0441-1
ISBN-13: 978-1-5095-0442-8 (pb)

A catalogue record for this book is available from the British Library.

Library of Congress Cataloging-in-Publication Data
Names: Sonn, Tamara, 1949- author.
Title: Is Islam an enemy of the west?/ Tamara Sonn.
Description: Cambridge, UK : Polity Press, 2016. | Includes bibliographical references and index.
Identifiers: LCCN 2016013754 (print) | LCCN 2016021309 (ebook) | ISBN 9781509504411 (hardback) | ISBN 9781509504428 (pbk.) | ISBN 9781509504442 (Mobi) | ISBN 9781509504459 (Epub)
Subjects: LCSH: Islam--2lst century. | Islam and politics. Terrorism--Religious aspects--Islam. | Jihad. | Islamic countries--Politics and government.
Classification: LCC BP161.3 .S66 2016 (print) | LCC BP161.3 (ebook) | DOC 297.09/05--dc23
LC record available at https://lccn.lcc.gov/201606013754

Typeset in 11 on 15 Sabon by
Servis Filmsetting Ltd, Stockport, Cheshire
Printed and bound in Great Britain by Clays Ltd, St Ives PLC

For further information on Polity, visit our website:
politybooks.com

Contents

To my family, with gratitude for their unwavering love and support.

Acknowledgments

Louise Knight of Polity Press deserves primary credit for both conceiving this book and convincing me to write it. I thank her, as well as Professor John L. Esposito and Professor John O. Voll, for their unwavering guidance and support. Special thanks go to Dr Gamal Heshmat, Dr Amr Darrag, Dr Hussein Elkazzaz, and Dr Yahya Hamed for clearly articulating the Muslim Brotherhood's objectives and strategies in their ongoing struggle for democracy, development, and the rule of law, and against terrorism. I would also like to thank Justin Dyer for his brilliant and painstaking editing of the manuscript. And special thanks go to my students at Georgetown University, who, by asking the right questions, helped me distill years of research and channel it into this very brief format.

1

Islam v. the West?

Is Islam an enemy of the West? It may sound like an odd question. How can an ancient global religion be an enemy of a modern geopolitical region? But if you pay attention to the news, there seem to be good reasons to think it is. Threats from terrorists claiming that their religion commands them to either convert or kill everyone are all over the cybersphere. And those threats started even before September 11, 2001, when 19 Arab terrorists attacked the United States. In 1996, al-Qaeda leader Osama bin Laden (d. 2011) published a "Declaration of War against the Americans Occupying the Land of the Two Holy Places," the cities Mecca and Medina, the birthplace of Islam, in his home country, Saudi Arabia. In 1998, he issued another message, this time ordering Muslims worldwide to kill Americans and their allies – both civilian and military – and to take their money, too. Bin Laden said this was the duty of every able-bodied Muslim in any country. American troops are doing the work of the devil, he said, and since the United States is a democracy, all Americans must be held responsible for their government's policies. Less than six months later, al-Qaeda operatives detonated truck bombs at two US embassies in Africa, killing over 200 people. After 9/11, Bin Laden was at it again, gloating over the successful attacks in New York and Washington, which killed nearly 3,000 people. They were followed by terrorist attacks in Madrid in 2004, which killed nearly 200, and in London in 2005, killing over 50 people. Though neither the Madrid nor London attacks were claimed by al-Qaeda, they were undoubtedly inspired by them. So if al-Qaeda represents Islam, it would seem that Islam is indeed an enemy of the West.

Since 9/11, anti-West Muslim groups appear to have multiplied. In 2002, the Nigerian terrorist group Boko Haram burst upon the scene. It started out demanding strict Islamic law in Muslim northern Nigeria, but within a few years it was calling for control of the whole country. In 2015, Boko Haram upped the ante yet again, announcing that Nigeria was only the beginning. From there it would expand across all of Africa and use it as a base to take over the entire world. Anyone who doesn't submit to Boko's law, said its leader Abubakar Shekau, has to either die or become a slave.

Boko Haram has pledged allegiance to the most successful terrorist group to date, Islamic State (formerly known as al-Qaeda in Iraq, ISIL, and ISIS, and also known as Daesh[1]). IS has taken control of territories in western Iraq and eastern Syria. Its leader, Abu Bakr al-Baghdadi, insists that his group is the vanguard for global Islamic domination. Islam, he says, is locked in a final showdown with "disbelief." The time for peace is over, al-Baghdadi declares; until the entire earth submits to Islamic law as he interprets it, Muslims must wield the sword. That is the way it must be, he says, until Judgment Day.

And it is not just twenty-first-century terrorist groups that have pledged war against the West. Every year the government of Iran commemorates the 1979 revolution that brought it to power, with loud public denunciations of America. *Marg bar Amrika!* – "Death to America!" – is their refrain. Leader of the 1979 revolution Ayatollah Khomeini (d. 1989) referred to the United States as "the Great Satan" – and that phrase caught on. It seemed to capture the idea that there was a single source behind all the problems facing Muslim countries, and that source is the United States. In fact, that was the inspiration behind Osama bin Laden's founding of al-Qaeda in the late 1980s. Instead of just working against specific Western allies like Egypt, Israel, and Saudi Arabia, al-Qaeda would go straight to the source. Muslims have a duty to fight the United States – that "monstrous" and "decadent" force – Bin Laden said, because it is, quite simply, "the worst civilization witnessed by the history of mankind."[2]

No wonder some far right politicians and commentators are able to argue that Islam is an enemy of the West. Dutch politician Geert Wilders has referred to the Qur'an, Islam's sacred scripture, as the Islamic *Mein Kampf*, and wants it banned in the Netherlands. Even before the current refugee crisis, he called for an end to Muslim immigration into Europe. Otherwise within 20 years, he said, Muslims will control the continent and impose their "sick" and "fascist" ideology. Wilders is convinced that Islam is indeed at war with the West. French politician Marine Le Pen seems to agree. Again, even before the Syrian refugee crisis, she was concerned about Muslim immigration from France's former colonies in North Africa, and compared it to the Nazi occupation during World War II. It may not be military occupation, said Le Pen, but Muslim immigration threatens the very survival of French civilization. American writer Robert Spencer offers similar advice to the United States. He warns that the US is preparing the way for its own destruction by allowing Muslims into the country. Maybe Islam didn't start out as a fascist religion, but over time, Spencer claims, it has become a "stealth" project. Its objective: to impose Islamic law on all Americans, making all non-Muslims "legal inferiors." Islam, Spencer asserts, is nothing short of a post-Nazi, post-Stalinist global totalitarian threat. In 2010, Spencer co-founded the American Freedom Defense Initiative with political activist Pamela Geller. Also known as Stop Islamization of America, the organization is the counterpart of Stop Islamization of Europe, founded in 2007 by Danish and English activists. The founders of these groups share the fear of a globalizing, fascist Islam, and feel compelled to awaken the world to the Islamic conspiracy. In 2015, right-wing American political commentator Glenn Beck published *It IS About Islam*, purporting to expose the true Islamic plan to take over the world. It is not just extremists who are the threat. Beck says Islam, the religion, and its scripture, the Qur'an, call for the subjugation of all non-Muslims and condemn them to hell. This is the reason for the "siege against America under way today."[3]

There is no reason to doubt that leaders of global terrorist organizations believe Islam commands them to fight the United States and its allies to the death. But there are good reasons not to believe that they represent Islam. For one thing, many Muslims are themselves Westerners. The first Muslims to come to America were African slaves, as far back as the sixteenth and seventeenth centuries. Today Muslims serve in US, Canadian, and European governments, and they are well represented in Western businesses, education, and the arts. Muslims comprise the second or third largest minorities in many Western countries. In addition, Western countries have strong bilateral relationships with numerous Muslim-majority countries. But the most obvious reason is that the vast majority of Muslims reject the claims of the terrorists. From 2001 to 2007, Gallup conducted the most extensive poll ever taken of Muslim public opinion worldwide (the results were published in 2007). Data from thousands of Muslims representing at least 90% of the global Muslim population showed that 93% condemned the 9/11 attacks as unjustified; the 7% who said they were justified gave political, not religious reasons for their views; and the majority said they admired many aspects of Western life.[4] These results have been replicated in numerous regional polls since then. In 2015, for example, a Pew Research poll was conducted, showing overwhelmingly negative views of Islamic State among Muslims.[5]

These public opinion polls reflect the views of mainstream Muslim religious authorities, who unanimously condemn terrorism. Although their statements don't make headlines the way terrorist proclamations do, Muslim religious authorities have repeatedly and publicly denounced terrorism ever since 9/11. University of North Carolina sociologist Charles Kurzman maintains a website[6] listing official statements against terrorism, beginning with a joint statement issued just days after 9/11. This included the views of leaders of Egypt's Muslim Brotherhood, Palestine's Hamas, Tunisia's al-Nahda Party, and their counterparts throughout the world. "We condemn in the strongest terms the incidents [of 9/11]," the authorities proclaim, "which are against all human and Islamic norms." The UNC site contains over 70 such joint condemnations, and links to many others. Numerous similar condemnations have been issued, most recently against Boko Haram and IS atrocities. They all hinge on the same principles: Islamic law forbids the killing of civilians, and the declaration of war by anyone but a duly recognized head of state – and even then it must be declared only as a last resort. Islamic law also forbids hostage taking, killing of political prisoners, the destruction of property, slavery, mistreatment of women, and forced conversions. Anti-terrorism statements by Muslims affirm Islam's commitment to protecting human rights, including religious freedom, and the sanctity of life.

So clearly, from the perspective of the vast majority of Muslims, the global terrorists are outliers, which explains the revealing fact that most of their victims are actually Muslims. This trend also began long before 9/11. One of the forerunners of al-Qaeda was an Egyptian terrorist organization that became infamous for assassinating President Anwar Sadat in 1981. That was a standard political assassination: the assassins condemned Sadat for his authoritarian ways, as well as his collaboration with the United States and Israel, despite the latter's illegal occupation of Palestinian territories. But the rationale offered by the assassins was unique: Sadat's political actions, they claimed, demonstrated that he was a Muslim in name only. So they declared him an apostate, deserving of death. The process of declaring professed Muslims to be apostates was banned in Islamic law over a thousand years ago, but its use by terrorists has increased in the past decade. This accounts for the massive killing by global terrorists of fellow Muslims in Afghanistan, Pakistan, Iraq, Syria, and Turkey.

But recognizing mainstream Muslims' condemnation of terrorist tactics should not obscure the fact that mainstream Muslims have some of the same political concerns expressed by the radicals. Like all formerly colonized countries, Muslim-majority countries have had to deal with stunted economic and political development, and the social problems that result from those challenges. There are nearly 50 Muslim-majority countries in the world, and almost all of them were victims of European imperialism. (Some still are: the Indian Ocean island of Mayotte is a part of France; Chechnya, home of the Boston Marathon bombers' family, is part of Russia; parts of traditional Morocco belong to Spain.) Most Muslim-majority countries did not get their independence until the mid-twentieth century, and often only with a great deal of effort. Yes, the petroleum industry has made some Muslims the richest people on earth, but those people are a fraction of the global Muslim population. Maldistribution is the name of the game. The richest states have the smallest populations. Oil-rich Abu Dhabi, for example, has under a half million citizens – fewer than Seattle or Dublin – and an *average* annual income of nearly $100,000 per person. But there are 1.6 billion Muslims in the world, nearly one quarter of the world's population. The majority of them live in oil-poor Asia. Pakistan, for example, has 185 million people; some of them are very rich, but the majority live on under $4 a day. Perhaps one-third of the world's Muslims live in Africa, where maldistribution is also a major issue. In Nigeria, Africa's largest country and home of Africa's richest man, the majority of the population lives on under $2 a day.

There are also areas where colonial-era conflicts remain unresolved: Palestine, occupied by Israel in violation of UN Security Council resolutions; Chechnya, controlled by Russia with an iron fist; and Kashmir, split between India and Pakistan while Kashmiris struggle for the chance to determine their own political future, for example. These are areas of concern to Muslims worldwide. Muslim majorities also share opposition to Western support for authoritarian governments, and to US-led wars in Afghanistan and Iraq.

Yet while mainstream and radical Muslims may share some concerns, there are significant differences between their two worldviews. For example, although mainstream Muslims believe the West shows little respect for their religion, the global terrorists see this as a "war on Islam" that justifies their anti-West campaigns.

An even more important distinction between mainstream Muslims and the radical fringe is in the strategies used by the former to address their concerns. Like any other people, Muslims want just and effective governance, and economic development. Most Muslims express support for representative governments, for government by consent of the governed, and for rule of law and human rights. They believe that these are in accordance with Islamic principles, and that Western policies often undermine those goals. But instead of attacking the West, the majority work through peaceful means at local, national, and international levels in order to achieve these goals.

The longer the struggle for economic and political development is prolonged, however, the more frustrated people become, leading some Muslims toward radicalization. There's a popular Palestinian hip-hop group, DAM (which means "blood" in Arabic), who rap about the irony of being accused of radicalism when they protest the illegal occupation of their land. In a famous line, they say that it was the rape of the Arab soul that spawned the suicide bomber. Indeed, Muslim public opinion views the morphing of national-level radicalism into international (global) jihadism – to say nothing of today's massive refugee crisis – as a direct result of the West's militarism, the "war on terror." There was, after all, no self-styled Islamic State before the 2003 US-led invasion of Iraq.

It should be emphasized, however, that the majority of Muslims are not radicalized. Understanding what motivates both terrorists and mainstream Muslims, and the profound differences between their objectives and strategies, helps make sense of the recent explosion of global jihadi groups, which only adds to the list of challenges faced by the majority. It also helps point toward effective means of counteracting the proliferation of global terrorist groups. Those are the issues we will examine, beginning with a profile of the jihadis' motivations and methods.

2

Jihad: Message, Motivation, and Methods

The year 2015 opened with terrorist attacks in Paris on January 7 in which two brothers killed 11 employees of *Charlie Hebdo* – a satirical magazine that had published insulting cartoons of Muhammad – as well as a policeman. The year closed with more attacks in Paris, this time killing 130 nighttime revelers on November 13, and a shooting at a Public Health Department facility in San Bernardino, California, on December 2, which killed 14 people. If any of these or countless others over the past 20 years represent Islam, then it seems that Islam is at war with the West. And that impression is intensified if you listen to the leaders of groups like al-Qaeda and its offshoot, Islamic State.

The first statement by one of those leaders, as noted in the previous chapter, came in 1996. Osama bin Laden, who had recently founded al-Qaeda, issued a "Declaration of War against the Americans Occupying the Land of the Two Holy Places." The focus of Bin Laden's anger was the Saudi ruling family, which he described as hopelessly corrupt and illegitimate because they didn't rule strictly in accordance with Islamic law. But the Saudis' ultimate offense, he said, was stationing US forces in the Arabian Peninsula. Not only was the expense of the US forces breaking the Saudi bank, according to Bin Laden, but these heathen "Crusader" forces were defiling the sacred Islamic heartland.

Why were US troops stationed in Saudi Arabia, and why was Bin Laden so angry about it? To answer this, we have to go back to 1979 and Iran, which underwent a major revolution in that year. A popular uprising ousted the Shah Mohamed Reza Pahlavi. The post-revolutionary government, headed by Ayatollah Khomeini, was very opposed to the West for its backing of the former king. During the revolution, a band of student activists occupied the US embassy, holding its personnel hostage for over a year. In response, the United States supported the invasion of Iran by its neighbor, Iraq, which was led by military dictator Saddam Hussein. Saddam was later overthrown by the United States, but at the time of the Iranian revolution, he was a major US ally. Iraq's invasion of Iran led to a bloody eight-year war; hundreds of thousands were killed on both sides. (Included among the arsenal used by Iraq were chemical weapons, whose components were sold to Saddam by US suppliers.) Throughout the war, Khomeini threatened to overthrow not just Saddam, but all governments in the region that cooperated with the West. That frightened the oil-rich Gulf states, especially Kuwait and Saudi Arabia. They supported Iraq's war effort to the tune of billions of dollars. When a ceasefire was finally declared in 1988, the Gulf states expected Saddam to pay back the funds they'd advanced, but he explained that he had been fighting not just for Iraq but on behalf of all the states threatened by revolutionary Iran; besides, after eight years of constant warfare, his economy was devastated and he couldn't pay back anything. Then, according to Iraqi sources, Kuwait began slant drilling under the border into Iraq's oil fields. Kuwait was historically part of Iraq – Britain had kept control of it (until 1961) when it granted the rest of Iraq independence in 1932. The two countries had never agreed on their borders, especially those running through rich oil fields. Saddam figured it was time to take back Kuwait and invaded. That was in 1990. The United States came to Kuwait's rescue in the following year and ejected Iraq's troops in the month-long Gulf War.

But the Saudis worried that they would be Saddam's next victim since he owed them money, too. By that time, the Soviet occupation of Afghanistan had ended. It had begun in the same year as the Islamic Revolution in Iran. In fact, at the same time the United States was helping Iraq defeat its enemy Iran, it was also helping Afghanistan defeat its archenemy the Soviet Union. With the help of allies, the United States trained and equipped countless volunteers streaming into Afghanistan to fight the Communists. Osama bin Laden, a Saudi citizen, was among them. After the defeat of the Soviets in 1988, most of the foreign volunteers had gone home. But some couldn't because they were wanted by their home governments. After some casting about, they decided to establish themselves as a group of warriors ready to fight whenever and wherever Muslims were under attack. They called themselves "the base" – "al-Qaeda" in Arabic. They weren't quite sure at first what their next job would be, but with the perceived threat from Saddam, Bin Laden's Saudi homeland seemed to be the place to start. So Bin Laden offered to bring his band of seasoned warriors home to protect Arabia from Iraq.

To his astonishment and outrage, the Saudi government rejected his offer. Instead, they accepted

American troops for the job. Welcoming these "infidels," Bin Laden claimed, amounted to desecration of the Muslim heartland, Mecca and Medina. That offense was compounded by what he called the Saudi rulers' "criminal" collaboration with the United States in its support for Israel. Since 1967, Israel has occupied Jerusalem – after Mecca and Medina, Islam's third holy city. The Saudi regime, Bin Laden said, had always promised to reunify the Muslim community, but instead they were allowing it to be further divided. They were buying arms from the United States, which he correctly identified as the major purveyor of weaponry in the region. They sold weapons not only to the Saudi government, but also to the Israelis, thus helping them "in occupying Palestine and in evicting and killing the Muslims there." Indeed, Bin Laden asserted, the Americans were purposely manipulating the rulers to keep Muslims fragmented and weak. The stationing of US troops, he claimed, was part of a "pre-planned military occupation" of Arabia. As proof, he quoted US Secretary of Defense William Perry, months before Bin Laden's 1996 declaration, saying that stationing US troops in Saudi Arabia would serve US interests. Thus, Bin Laden said, the Saudi regime was collaborating with enemies of Islam.

That is when Bin Laden had focused on the United States as the one target all his warriors could agree on. Soon afterwards came the first al-Qaeda-inspired attack on New York's World Trade Center (1993), which killed six people and injured over a thousand. In 1996, Bin Laden called on Muslims to "[cleanse] our sanctities from the Crusaders [Americans] and Zionists [Israelis] and [force] them ... to leave, disappointed and defeated." The Saudi regime is culpable, he said, but the "occupying American enemy is the principal and main cause of the situation. Therefore, efforts should be concentrated on destroying, fighting and killing the enemy until ... it is completely defeated." Bin Laden's message then praised those who had participated in recent terrorist attacks on US military targets in the Saudi cities of Riyadh and Khobar. He recounted the suffering of Muslims under Israeli occupation in Palestine and Russian occupation in Chechnya and the unpopular pro-Russian government in Tajikistan, among other places, and issued a call to jihad. He expressed hatred for all those who caused suffering to Muslims, but said young Muslim men must primarily focus on fighting the Americans and the Israelis.[1]

This focus on a single enemy deemed the mastermind behind local conflicts was unprecedented in Islamic history. In fact, it violated the Qur'an's command to fight only those who directly attack – the "near enemy" (2:192–4; 9:123). But Osama bin Laden was not a religious authority. He had no formal religious education; his university training was in civil engineering. He could say whatever he wanted about politics, but he had no authority to call on Muslims to do anything in the name of religion. That didn't bother him, however. Five months before the 1998 al-Qaeda bombings of US embassies in Tanzania and Kenya, Bin Laden issued what he called a fatwa – an authoritative religious opinion. This time he found four religious scholars to countersign. In it he rehearsed the complaints against the United States and Israel, again describing the US military presence in Arabia as an occupation. He then moved on to the sanctions against Iraq.

Sanctions had been imposed on Iraq by the international community, led by the United States, after the Gulf War of 1991. By the time of Bin Laden's 1998 fatwa, the sanctions had led to mass starvation among Iraqis. Bin Laden called attention to reports of half a million children dying as a result. He played on worldwide outrage, particularly in the wake of a televised 1996 CBS interview in which then Secretary of State Madeleine Albright was asked about the tragic death toll, citing the same UN Food and Agriculture Organization statistics Bin Laden had used. Albright responded that it was a difficult situation but that the administration thought the deaths were "a price worth paying." Albright later expressed regret for the statement but it was too late. It had already ricocheted around the world. In characteristically melodramatic language, Bin Laden's 1998 fatwa claimed that "the Crusader–Zionist alliance" was trying "to annihilate what is left of this people and to humiliate their Muslim neighbors."

And again Bin Laden returned to US support for Israel despite its continued violation of UN Security Council resolutions. For him, there was no difference between actual combat and foreign policy. The stationing of troops, sanctions, political alliances – it was all war to Bin Laden, and not just any war: it was religious war. Ignoring the existence of Palestinian Christians, Bin Laden claimed, "All these crimes and sins committed by the Americans are a clear declaration of war on [God], his messenger, and Muslims." Therefore, he concluded, fighting the United States is a matter of self-defense.[2]

After the terrorist attacks on the United States on September 11, 2001 and the subsequent US-led invasion of Afghanistan, Bin Laden issued another statement addressed specifically to Americans. He reminded the United States of the "holy warriors" – the Mujahideen – and their success in defeating the Soviets in Afghanistan. He said that the Muslims were able "to destroy the previous evil empire [the Soviet Union]" and that the United States was just like it. He warned the Americans that they must quit their evil ways; if they didn't, the Muslims were prepared to fight them. "You are well aware that the Islamic Nation," he said, "from the very core of its soul, despises your haughtiness and arrogance."[3]

Bin Laden was assassinated in a US operation in March 2011, but this didn't end the threat; indeed, his successors among global jihadis have become even more radical. Al-Qaeda wants to bring down the United States. Ultimately, its adherents want to establish a caliphate in the Arabian peninsula (they don't like using the name "Saudi" Arabia) and, from there, to reunify all Muslims. But that is a distant goal. First they believe they must destroy the United States. They take on special assignments when the occasion presents itself – like fighting the Syrian government in that country's civil war. And they are willing to attack US allies in their campaign against the United States. But they're basically warriors, not administrators. The next generation of international terrorists is a different story. They see no reason to wait for the opportunity to claim territory. They take whatever opportunity presents itself. That generation is represented by a group that began as an al-Qaeda franchise after the US-led invasion of Iraq in 2003: since 2014 they have called themselves Islamic State.

There have been groups calling for reestablishment of the caliphate – the Islamic equivalent of the medieval papacy, envisioned as a religio-political authority – since it was abolished after World War I. That's when the Ottoman Empire – seat of the last caliphate – was dismantled and dismembered. Its heartland became Turkey, and the rest of it – stretching throughout the Arab Middle East and across North Africa – was taken over by Britain, France, and Italy (which took control of Libya). During the middle of the twentieth century, these areas became the modern Arab countries of the Middle East and North Africa. But other groups calling for a new caliphate have not been militant and have not attracted large followings. The self-styled Islamic State (IS) is quite different. It calls for the reestablishment of the caliphate now – and not just as a symbol of Islamic religious unity; its goal is a unified Islamic geopolitical entity. And it calls for achieving that goal not just through moral persuasion but by force, including force against Muslims who resist it. Thanks to the breakdown of the Iraqi military following the 2003 US invasion and the civil war in Syria, IS has actually been able to conquer a significant amount of territory spanning the border between Iraq and Syria. This represents a new level in international terrorism – al-Qaeda 2.0. But this new generation shares with its parent al-Qaeda a virulent hatred of the West.

Hatred of the West, including Jews, has obviously been identified as an effective marketing tool by terrorists. Fiery audio clips from IS leader Abu Bakr al-Baghdadi are translated and widely disseminated by the group's professional e-media arm to recruit warriors against the West. In a famous announcement in July 2014, al-Baghdadi ordered Muslims to "[s]tand up and rise. For the time has come for you to free yourself from the shackles of weakness, and stand in the face of tyranny, against the treacherous rulers – the agents of the Crusaders [Christians] and the atheists, and the guards of the Jews!" Swearing to take vengeance on the whole world for offenses against Muslims everywhere from Central Africa to Burma, al-Baghdadi declared that he has reestablished the caliphate to rule over all Muslims in a utopian paradise. The state he has established in Iraq and Syria is just the beginning.[4]

Responses to al-Baghdadi's proclamation from leaders throughout the Muslim world were negative. The popular Sunni scholar Yusuf al-Qaradawi, for example, was quoted dismissing the declaration as dangerous, and with no validity in Islamic law. But al-Baghdadi remained undeterred. He went right on recruiting. Less than a year later, he issued a new call for all true Muslims to carry on the battle against Jews, Christians, those he considers insincere Muslims, "and other disbelievers," wherever they are. He warns "true" Muslims that they will never be able to reconcile or live in peace with such people, so they must take action. They must come and join him in his self-styled Islamic state, just as the first generation of Muslims followed the Prophet Muhammad from Mecca to Medina. Most Muslims consider that journey – known as the *hijra* (emigration) – to have been a one-time event, some 1,400 years ago. But al-Baghdadi disagrees. He argues that *hijra* is emigration from any non-Muslim country to his version of a properly ruled Muslim polity, and that this emigration is an ever-present duty for all Muslims. Furthermore, most Muslims believe that war – jihad – can be declared only by a duly recognized head of state and only as a last resort. But in al-Baghdadi's view, jihad is also an ever-present duty incumbent upon all Muslims.

And it is not to be fought just for self-defense, as most Muslims believe. For the IS leader, jihad is the command to fight "unbelievers" – non-Muslims and "false" Muslims – regardless of whether they have initiated hostilities or not. The command for true believers to undertake both *hijra* and jihad is valid, says al-Baghdadi, until the day Jesus returns to earth to usher in the End Times. (Yes, Muslims believe Jesus will come again to prepare things for the final triumph of good over evil.) In fact, in his apocalyptic perspective, the End Times are nigh. It's the apocalypse now; good must triumph over evil once and for all. "[T]he battle is one between the allies of the Merciful [God] and the allies of Satan."

For al-Baghdadi, Muslims are on a collision course with the forces of evil incarnate: the West and everyone else who does not join their battle. While Bin Laden thought the West could be corrected if it only changed its course, for the leader of IS, it's too late for that. The forces of good and evil are finally going to fight to the death, Good will triumph, and all those who join them will be rewarded eternally while the rest suffer the excruciating pain that sinners deserve. It is a universal struggle; no one will be spared.[5]

Islam against Muslims

So if the leaders of al-Qaeda and IS represent Islam, then, yes, Islam is an enemy of the West. But that's a very big "if," for a number of reasons. One, as mentioned in the previous chapter, is that the vast majority of victims of terrorism are Muslims. In order to establish their stronghold in Iraq/Syria, IS had to battle Iraqi and Syrian forces, and subjugate civilian populations. The civilian death toll alone in Iraq since the rise of IS, according to the only group that is really counting – Iraq Body Count – is over 174,000 (as of March 2016). Of that number, it is impossible to determine what portion is attributable to IS, but a UN Human Rights Office report issued after the fall of Mosul to IS in June 2014 identified nearly 10,000 civilian deaths – Muslim and Christian, with IS identified as responsible for the majority. Since the beginning of the Syrian civil war in 2011, there have been an estimated 250,000 civilian deaths. The vast majority are attributed to the Syrian government's attacks on its own people. That may explain why some communities have been willing to submit to IS domination; IS may appear to be the only effective force against Assad. But more revealingly, nearly 5 million Syrians have become refugees since 2011, rather than submit to the brutality of either the Assad regime or the IS alternative. And Islamic State affiliate in Nigeria Boko Haram is even more deadly than IS, according to the latest Global Terrorism Index report. Calling itself ISWAP (Islamic State's West Africa Province) since March 2015, Boko Haram is credited with killing over 6,600 people in 2014, compared with just over 6,000 attributed to IS. The report confirms that the vast majority of terrorist attacks take place not in the West but in Muslim-majority countries convulsed by civil war, and that the vast majority of victims are therefore Muslim.[6]

Overall, statistics about the religious identities of victims of terrorist attacks are difficult to come by, for the obvious reason that rescue workers and medical teams have other priorities. They are too busy doing triage to take surveys about religion. But a 2011 report issued by the US National Counterterrorism Center claimed: "In cases where the religious affiliation of terrorism casualties could be determined, Muslims suffered between 82 and 97 percent of terrorism-related fatalities over the past five years."[7] So it should come as no surprise that, as a 2014 Pew Research Center Global Attitudes and Trends poll indicated, Muslims are as concerned as everyone else about terrorism, and increasing majorities hold very negative opinions of specific groups such as al-Qaeda, Hamas, Hezbollah, Boko Haram, and the Taliban. In Lebanon, for instance, 92% register concern about terrorism, an 11% increase since 2013.[8]

Legal scholar Cherif Bassiouni summarizes: "Muslims have suffered the most from the wrongful, violent practices and erroneous or misleading religious beliefs held by some Muslims . . . ." Writing in 2015, he said that over 300,000 Muslims have been killed in Iraq, for example, compared with perhaps 20,000 Christians. Bassiouni reports that IS executed nearly 2,000 people in the last six months of 2014 alone, while in Nigeria Boko Haram killed more than that number in the town of Baga in a single day.[9]

Why do the terrorists kill Muslims if their main enemies are the West? The answer to that question is the main reason not to assume that al-Qaeda and IS represent Islam. It is that the majority of Muslims reject terrorism. Not only do the vast majority of Muslims reject terrorism under any circumstances – more than non-Muslim Americans do, in fact – but the terrorists are well aware that most Muslims reject them.

Jihadis are outliers

The global jihadis who consider themselves in a death match with a generic "West" are also in a death match with the majority of Muslims, because they know the majority disagree with them. As noted in the previous chapter, the jihadis are outliers within Islam and take pride in that status. They actually condemn the majority of Muslims. There are two basic kinds of Muslims – Sunni and Shia (or Shiite). They agree on most things but split into separate groups about 1,300 years ago over how to choose the leader of the community. Today over 85% of Muslims are Sunni and the rest are Shia. But the extreme radicals reject the Shia as heretics. And they call Sunnis who fail to join their cause hypocrites or worse: apostates deserving of death.

Among the radicals' major strategists was Abu Bakr al-Naji (d. 2008; pseudonym of Muhammad Khalil al-Hakaymah, also known as Abu Jihad al-Masri). In a hugely influential 2004 online publication, *The Management of Savagery*, al-Naji laid out a detailed strategy for guerrilla warfare, reckoning the need for half a million warriors. But, he warned, "the masses" could not be depended upon; their minds had been "polluted" by mainstream preachers in the service of tyrants. Media outreach was therefore important in order to "neutralize" the Muslim masses and draw out the few "elect" from the rest. They would be from among uncultivated youths whose "rebellious nature" had not been tamed through mainstream education.[10]

Al-Naji repeatedly condemns the founder of Egypt's Muslim Brotherhood, Hassan al-Banna (d. 1949), for rejecting terrorism and especially for rejecting the targeting of civilians. He's convinced that terrorist attacks of escalating destructiveness will impress civilians and win them over to the jihadi cause. Al-Naji also insists that jihadis must target not just the foreigners in Muslim lands but also those Muslims who cooperate with them in any way. Anyone who cooperates with the Americans has joined "the Crusaders" and is therefore an apostate and should be targeted. Al-Naji is well aware that Islamic law prohibits both declaring Muslims apostates and killing civilians, so he tries to argue against those prohibitions. He says that all Muslims who don't join him are nothing short of traitors. If they are not with us, then they are against us, he says. "Thus," he concludes, "there is nothing preventing us from spilling their blood; rather, we see that this is one of the most important obligations since they do not repent, undertake prayer, and give alms."

Probably the best-known global jihadi strategist is Abu Mus`ab al-Suri ("the Syrian"; pseudonym of Mustafa Sitmariam Nasar, also known as Umar Abd al-Hakim; b. 1958). His magnum opus *Da`wat al-Muqawamat al-Islamiyyat al-`Alamiyyah* (The Call to Global Islamic Resistance) also appeared online after the US-led invasion of Iraq. Unlike al-Naji, al-Suri doesn't think Shia Muslims should be targeted. Doctrinal differences should be left to the experts, he says. But like al-Naji, al-Suri condemns all non-jihadi Muslims and non-militant Islamists, including the Muslim Brotherhood. And also like al-Naji, he calls for dramatic terrorist exploits, especially suicide attacks, because he thinks they will inspire everyone and persuade the majority of Muslims that they should switch sides. Al-Suri and al-Naji both fought in the Afghan jihad against Soviet occupation during the 1980s. They also both benefited from training provided by Arab regimes, including Egypt and Iraq. But al-Suri now believes that cooperating with existing regimes is a mistake. He says that jihadis must never again rely on Arab governments because they want to use them to advance their own geopolitical agendas. He claims that Arab governments' intelligence operatives infiltrated the jihadi ranks and were able to then control various members of the organizations through blackmail and "security traps." By means of these techniques, he asserts, unnamed Arab governments demanded "favors" and interfered with their plans.[11] So again, al-Suri says, it doesn't matter if most Muslims reject the jihadis. Actually, it's better that way, he argues, because then they can be their own bosses. But in order to maintain their autonomy, they have to keep strict secrecy. They should only meet in small groups, preferably in private homes, and set up training only in top-secret areas. In other words, he says, the jihadis are outsiders and they must stay that way.

In fact, being the outsiders – "rebels with a cause" – is a major recruiting tool for the jihadis. IS leader al-Baghdadi issued a message in late 2014 whose title can be loosely translated as "So What If the [Mainstream Muslims] Hate [Our Call to Global Jihad]?" The message acknowledges that most Muslims condemn their tactics, but he explains that that's because they're gullible. They've been brainwashed by mainstream Muslim religious authorities – whom al-Baghdadi calls "criminal sorcerers." He ridicules them as being "effeminate," "dogs" and "slaves" of the West. They're being humiliated and disgraced by the West, which controls their resources and occupies their land, and they don't even care. Who would want to be accepted by such degenerates? It is those rejected and spurned by the degenerate elites who are truly noble, say IS recruiters.

Predictions of triumph over retrograde elites are purposely pitched to the marginalized under-class, the unemployed, and especially those who feel rejected by the mainstream. Highly produced online materials target audience's frustrations and the desire for vengeance against the world that seems to have rejected them. Studies based on interviews with captured IS fighters show that most express a strong sense of alienation from their environments, and discontent with their social and political status. Most revealing is the fact that, proportionately, Western Muslims – who feel the sting of discrimination in White Christian-majority countries – are 100 times more likely to be successfully recruited that those living in Muslim-majority communities.

Al-Qaeda and IS also carefully train personal recruiters who work among target audiences. A 2010 online recruiting manual based on al-Suri's teachings ("A Course in the Art of Recruiting" by Abu Amru al-Qa`idi) begins with a very revealing directive.[12] Recruiters are instructed to target only people who aren't very religious. And don't even try to recruit people who know very much about Islam, recruiters are told. If they're religious or know much about Islam, they'll probably think jihadis violate Islamic norms. The manual warns that they'll ask probing questions about 9/11 and the killing of innocent people. They might even think it's the jihadis' fault that so many people have a negative view of Islam and insult Muhammad in cartoons. So recruiters are advised to target people who are non-religious or even irreligious, or those who have just begun a religious journey. Recruiters are also advised that high school students are preferable to college people, who ask too many questions. In fact, youths from rural areas are preferable to urban kids. The less sophisticated the better. And when recruiters see their potential recruits engaging in un-Islamic behavior, they're told not to be too critical. Instead, give them gifts and show interest in their activities. Take every occasion to let them know of terrible things that happen to Muslims due to Western policies. The manual explains that not all Muslims share the same concerns, but everyone knows about the injustices suffered by Palestinians, it says, so recruiters should focus on Palestine. And if potential recruits begin to ask technical questions about Islamic law, recruiters are instructed not to defer to authorities. Just tell them that jihad is their personal responsibility, and remind them of the beauties waiting for them in Paradise. Do not complicate their lives with details of law; give them some simple prayers to repeat in order to gain spiritual rewards, and some simple practices like following the dental hygiene routine established by Muhammad. Tell them this will help them become better Muslims.

Recruiters are also told to hold off on introducing potential inductees to their slick online videos depicting violence until they're ready. Recruiters are warned that the violence might repulse them until they have been sufficiently motivated to seek revenge against the perpetrators of evil. Their videos are violent indeed, and increasingly so. While some resemble blockbuster Hollywood disaster films – and may actually steal footage from them – others are grisly in the extreme. Showing scenes of beheadings and immolations, they have been described as death-porn. These are particularly effective for urban kids bred on the most violent online games; others may need some preparatory work.

But most importantly, recruiters are told, remind potential volunteers that although they may feel like outsiders and misfits, they are not alone. They will find a home if they just sign up for jihad.

More Maoist than Muslim

It is not surprising that the majority of Muslims find the radicals' methods unorthodox. Jihadis' manuals actually focus far more on strategic matters – how to defeat their enemies – than they do on religious issues. And although they frequently cite religious motivations for their campaign, their strategies and tactics are consciously based on guerrilla warfare methods developed by the likes of Mao Tse-tung, Che Guevara, and General Vo Nguyen Giap, leader of the forces that defeated both the French and the United States in Vietnam. All are mentioned frequently, as is nineteenth-century Prussian military theorist Carl von Clausewitz (of "War is a continuation of politics by other means" fame). US manuals dealing with "4GW" – Fourth-Generation Warfare (warfare by non-state actors and therefore using terrorist tactics) – are also frequently cited.

Among the most influential global jihadi strategists is a former Bin Laden advisor known as Abu Ubayd al-Qurashi, who published a series of articles online in 2002–3. In the first one, titled "Revolutionary War," al-Qurashi describes measures by which "the weak" will be able to defeat "the strong," a non-state group will be able to overthrow an established government, and replace it with a new one based on a new ideology. Terrorism is effective in this process, claims al-Qurashi, but he cautions that too much terrorism will cause a backlash against the movement, as happened, he says, in Greece in 1947. So it is critical to the success of the movement to learn from Chairman Mao, from whom he quotes: "War cannot be separated even for a second from politics." The people must know the political objectives of the campaign. And they must feel some benefit. Again quoting Mao, he advises the jihadis to treat people well during their operations. Do not steal from people or rape their women, he says, citing Che Guevara as a prime model of this approach. Finally, al-Qurashi argues that in order for people to accept terrorism, it has to be presented to them as a battle for justice against tyranny. In perhaps his most revealing statement, al-Qurashi says, "[W]ithout the agreement and support of the people, the revolutionary movement will be no more than a gang of criminals."[13] Tellingly, the article compares guerrilla warriors' struggle to that of David fighting Goliath and mentions that the battle will go on until Judgment Day – but it contains no mention of Islam.

The strategist known as al-Suri also advocates Chairman Mao's methods. Like al-Qurashi, he refers to a book titled after Mao's analogy for guerrilla warfare. Guerrilla warfare, said Mao, is like the "war of the flea" – endless random flea bites that cause a dog to scratch himself into a state of exhaustion. Then all that's needed are a few final blows and the beast succumbs. Published in 1965, *War of the Flea* was written not by a Muslim strategist but by American journalist Robert Taber, and al-Suri calls it the best book ever written about guerrilla warfare.

It is clear that these strategists influenced Bin Laden as early as his 1996 statement condemning the presence of US troops in Arabia. After a long discussion of the injustices committed by the United States and its allies, Saudi Arabia and Israel, Bin Laden says that "due to the imbalance of power ... a suitable means of fighting must be adopted." That means guerrilla warfare, which he describes as "fast moving light forces that work under complete secrecy." As if he had read Mao himself, Bin Laden called upon Muslim communities to support the guerrilla warriors, giving them information and material support, spreading rumors to discourage and frighten the enemy, and, most importantly, covering up for the guerrillas when the security services ask about them.[14]

So jihadis consciously self-identify as outsiders, and rely on non-Muslim sources as they strategize their attacks against both the West and mainstream Muslims. They are both ideological and numerical minorities. Intelligence estimates as of September 2015 indicate successful recruitment of around 30,000 foreign fighters and the establishment of dozens of foreign branches. Their Islam is undoubtedly hostile to the West. But it is also hostile to mainstream Muslims, whom the terrorists condemn and who comprise the majority of their victims. Therefore, it's no surprise that the majority of Muslims are opposed to the terrorists – a subject to which we now turn.

3

Muslim Opposition to Terror

Many people have heard the term "Islamist" and equate it with any Muslims who use Islamic terms of reference in political discourse. But there are important differences between generic Muslims and mainstream Islamists, on the one hand, and jihadi Islamists, on the other. Generic Muslims, like people in general, go about their lives the best they can. They participate to the extent possible in whatever political environment they live in. "Islamist" is a generic term for Muslims who believe their religious values should inform not just private issues such as worship and family matters, but political and economic issues as well. The oldest Islamist organization is the Muslim Brotherhood, founded in Egypt in 1928. The Muslim Brotherhood spread to neighboring Arab countries, including Sudan and Jordan, but each organization focuses on issues pertinent to its own country. It is not an organization with an international agenda. Moreover, the Muslim Brotherhood is non-militant; its members participate in political processes, advocating the rule of law, democratic governance, separation of powers, and transparency. All of these are believed to be Islamic. Mainstream Muslims and Islamists alike reject unauthorized violence as a political tool. That is why the jihadis – those who do insist on violence as the ultimate political tool – are enemies of mainstream Islam. As terrorism expert Michael W.S. Ryan puts it, "In fact, nonviolent Islamists like the current Muslim Brotherhood in Egypt are among the greatest threat to al-Qaeda's ideology."[1]

Popular opposition to terror

Mainstream Muslim opposition to terrorism is evident in surveys of popular opinion. A 2007 World Public Opinion survey showed overwhelming rejection of terrorist attacks and the organizations that perpetrate them in Indonesia, Pakistan, and Egypt, for example. So strong is the rejection of terrorism that many Muslims express skepticism that Muslims could have actually perpetrated the 9/11 attacks.[2]

As noted in Chapter 1, the comprehensive Gallup World Poll survey of Muslim public opinion between 2001 and 2007 indicated that 93% of Muslims believe the 9/11 attacks were unjustified.[3] This contrasts with public opinion in North America (surveyed by Gallup in 2008–10), where only 50% view military attacks on civilians as wholly unjustified, and 49% say they are sometimes justified. In Europe, 61% say such attacks are never justified, while 19% say they are sometimes justified. What about non-military groups targeting civilians? That group would include both terrorists and "contract" fighters or mercenaries. The 2008–10 Gallup poll indicates that 85% of respondents in the Middle East and North Africa believe such attacks are never justified, and 9% that they are sometimes justified. This contrasts with 69% of Europeans and 77% of North Americans believing they are never justified; 12% of Europeans and 21% of North Americans believe non-military attacks on civilians are sometimes justified.[4]

Religious authorities' opposition to terror

Islamic thought is far from monolithic; there is no official clergy in the religion. Like Judaism, its normative positions are formed by religious authorities trained in the religion's vast legal heritage. Nor is there a single body of religious authorities. The authorities of (majority) Sunni Islam are trained in diverse schools of thought. Each of them has a range of approaches, from conservative to progressive. Shia Muslims make up the rest of the world's Muslims, and they are also diverse. (The religious authorities of the majority of Shia – Ithna`ashari or "Twelver" – are sometimes referred to as clergy, given their hierarchical ranking based on degrees of training. Ayatollahs represent the highest rank of Twelver Shia training, and there are several of them at any given time.) Despite this diversity, there is significant overlap among Muslim religious authorities on major issues. The sanctity of life and rules concerning legal warfare are among them. Both of those issues are central to Muslim religious authorities' condemnations of terrorism.

Terrorism has been the subject of countless condemnations by Muslim authorities since 9/11. Nor is condemnation of terrorism a new phenomenon in Islamic law, whereas in the United States terrorism was defined and criminalized only in the late twentieth century (US Criminal Code Title 18, Part I, Ch. 113B, 1993, with subsequent amendments). The term used for terrorism in Islamic law is *hirabah*, an offense with strict mandatory punishments since Islam's earliest days. Islamic law, generically known as Sharia, has a set of agreed-upon objectives. Despite the dynamism and diversity present in Sharia, virtually all authorities concur that its objectives include preservation of life, religion, family, property, and human dignity. These are called the basic rights of human beings. There are long discussions and variations of opinion regarding the best ways to preserve these human rights. And opinions vary on whether the primary value is the sanctity of life or religion, since it is permissible to take a life in a just war, but it is also permissible to defer religious obligations in order to save a life. But there is no disagreement that life is sacred in Islamic law. That sanctity is at the root of Islam's prohibition of terrorism.

Islam's definition of *hirabah* is broader than Western definitions of terrorism. In US law, terrorism involves violent acts intended to intimidate a civilian population, or to influence the policy or conduct of government. In Islamic law, terrorism involves violence against random victims. The rationale is simple. In classical Islamic law, just as in Mosaic law, the basic means of preventing personal injury crimes was the principle of reciprocity: an eye for an eye, a tooth for a tooth, a life for a life.

But the assumption was that if someone commits one of these crimes, it's against an enemy. There was an argument over some insult, for example, or a property dispute, or someone stole someone else's wife. People didn't have to worry that they might be the next victims because they knew that the attacker's grievance was against the particular person he attacked. But *hirabah* was something different. *Hirabah* attacks were against random victims. Whereas modern Western law assumes political objectives in terrorist attacks, Islamic law requires no such motive. It assumes personal gain as a motive, since it was usually in the commission of robbery, for example, that *hirabah* was committed. But the motivation is not the critical element in Sharia's prohibition of terrorism. It is the randomness of its victims. If someone can be attacked without provocation, then anyone can be attacked without provocation. In other words, no one feels safe.

Random victimization is such a grievous crime in Islamic law because the overall objective of Islamic law – what those human rights are meant to bring about – is social well-being. That well-being is actually related to the root meaning of the term *islam*, which is "peace," as in the common Muslim greeting *as-salaam alaykum*, "Peace be with you."

It doesn't mean just "peace" as in the "absence of war," but peace in the sense of security and well-being. For that reason, *hirabah* is considered the opposite of *islam*. In fact, it is described by classical Muslim scholars as a crime that results in "fear in the streets." In other words, *hirabah* involves actions that bring about terror in the populace; it is terrorism. Because it is the opposite of the peace and security that Islam is meant to bring, terrorism is universally condemned by Muslim religious authorities.

Terrorist attacks committed by Muslims in the United States began, as we noted in the previous chapter, in 1993, with the first bombing of New York's World Trade Center. That attack claimed six lives. The next al-Qaeda attack was against the housing complex of US troops stationed in Saudi Arabia in 1996. That attack killed 20. As noted in Chapter 2, US personnel were also attacked in East Africa in 1998, killing 224. The attack on the US Navy destroyer USS *Cole* in Yemen in 2000 killed 17. These attacks resulted in thousands of injuries, as well. But, as atrocious as all these casualties were, it was only with the 9/11 attacks in New York and Washington DC in 2001 that terrorist strikes against the United States resulted in civilian deaths and injuries of truly massive proportions. Moreover, on this occasion, a Muslim group publicly claimed responsibility and also declared that the attacks were justified. Both the horrific magnitude of the 9/11 attacks and the assertion that they were somehow justified led to immediate and resounding public condemnations by Muslim authorities. Since that time, and despite repeated claims that Muslims do not speak out against terrorism, the record is clear. Muslim authorities of every variety – diverse Sunnis and Shia – have repeatedly and publicly condemned terrorism as crimes against both Islam and humanity at large.

On September 12, 2001, the leader of the organization that represents the world's 57 Muslim-majority or near-majority countries, the Organization of the Islamic Cooperation, issued a press release condemning "those criminal and brutal acts" and stating that they were "counter to all covenants, humanitarian values and divine religions, foremost among which [is] Islam."

On September 13, the most popular Sunni religious authority in the world, Yusuf al-Qaradawi, stated that despite his opposition to many US policies, he was heartbroken by the attacks of 9/11, adding that Islam "holds the human soul in high esteem, and considers the attack against innocent human beings a grave sin." He quoted the Qur'an:

"Whosoever kills a human being [as punishment] for [crimes] other than manslaughter or corruption on earth, it shall be as if he has killed all mankind, and whosoever saves the life of one, it shall be as if he had saved the life of all of mankind" (Surah al-Ma'idah 5:32). (The same day, the British musician formerly known as Cat Stevens, Yusuf Islam, issued a press release expressing his horror at the attacks. "We pray for the families of all those who lost their lives in this unthinkable act of violence as well as all those injured; I hope to reflect the feelings of all Muslims and people around the world whose sympathies go out to the victims at this sorrowful moment.")

Three days after 9/11, the leaders of Egypt's Muslim Brotherhood, Pakistan's and Bangladesh's major Islamist organization the Jamaat-e-Islami, Palestine's Hamas (an acronym for "Islamic Resistance Movement"), Tunisia's al-Nahda Party, and over 40 other groups published the following statement in London's *al-Quds al-Arabi* newspaper:

> The undersigned, leaders of Islamic movements, are horrified by the events of Tuesday 11 September 2001 in the United States which resulted in massive killing, destruction and attack on innocent lives. We express our deepest sympathies and sorrow. We condemn, in the strongest terms, the incidents, which are against all human and Islamic norms.

> This is grounded in the Noble Laws of Islam which forbid all forms of attacks on innocents. God Almighty says in the Holy Qur'an: "No bearer of burdens can bear the burden of another" (Surah al-Isra 17:15).

On the same day, Muhammad Sayyid al-Tantawi, the leader of Sunni Islam's premier university, Al-Azhar in Cairo, issued a statement that declared: "Attacking innocent people is not courageous; it is stupid and will be punished on the day of judgment … ." In a similar vein, the leader of Lebanon's Hezbollah, Muhammad Hussein Fadlallah, told Agence France Presse that the 9/11 attacks were barbaric crimes that are forbidden by Islam. "Islamists who live according to the human values of Islam could not commit such crimes."

On September 16, the American Muslim Political Coordination Council took out a full-page ad in *The Washington Post* in order to promulgate the many condemnations of terrorism by Muslim authorities. It included their statement: "American Muslims utterly condemn what are apparently vicious and cowardly acts of terrorism against innocent civilians. We join with all Americans in calling for the swift apprehension and punishment of perpetrators. No political cause could ever be assisted by such immoral acts."

Countless statements condemning terrorism in general and 9/11 in particular were issued in the following weeks and months. In December 2001, a member of Saudi Arabia's Council of Senior Religious Scholars, Muhammad bin `Abdullah al-Sabil, said, "Any attack on innocent people is unlawful and contrary to Sharia. ... Muslims must safeguard the lives, honor, and property of Christians and Jews. Attacking them contradicts Sharia."

The US-led invasion of Iraq in 2003 led to al-Qaeda-style attacks on European coalition partners. On March 11, 2004, bombs detonated on four commuter trains during rush hour in Madrid killed 191 people and injured over 1,500. Again, Muslim authorities issued condemnations. In May 2004, for example, the chairman of the Supreme Judicial Council of Saudi Arabia issued a public statement proclaiming that such terrorist acts as 9/11 and Spain's 3/11 were "pernicious and shameless evils which are not justified by any sane logic, nor by the religion of Islam." But it was obvious that the message was not getting through. US-led military activities continued in Afghanistan and Iraq, further convincing the terrorists that they needed to defeat the "Crusaders" and all Muslims who disagreed with jihadism. They stepped up their attacks on both military and civilian targets. In November 2004, King Abdullah of Jordan issued a comprehensive condemnation of terrorism signed by 200 Muslim authorities, Sunni and Shia, from 50 countries. Their proclamation, the Amman Message, which has been signed by hundreds more authorities since its original issuance, began by affirming the diversity of viewpoints in Islam and the validity of Sunni, Shia, and other approaches to Islamic practice. It reasserted Islam's classical prohibition of *takfir* – the designation of a professed Muslim as an apostate deserving of capital punishment. It also confirmed human rights, including the rights of women and minorities, freedom of religion, the citizenship responsibilities of Muslims living in non-Muslim countries, and Islam's commitment to self-determination and the right to choose democratic governance. With regard to terrorism, the Amman Message said:

> Islam recognizes the noble station of [human] life, so there is to be no fighting against non-combatants, and no assault upon civilians and their properties, children at their mothers' bosom, students in their schools, nor upon elderly men and women. Assault upon the life of a human being, be it murder, injury or threat, is an assault upon the right to life among all human beings. It is among the gravest of sins;

for human life is the basis for the prosperity of humanity.

On the first anniversary of the Madrid attack, the Islamic Commission of Spain issued a fatwa directly against Osama Bin Laden, claiming, "Muslims ... are not only forbidden from committing crimes against innocent people, but are responsible before God to stop those people who have the intention to do so ... ." The fatwa took the controversial step of claiming that terrorist acts are so profound a violation of Islamic norms that "the individuals or groups who have perpetrated them have stopped being Muslim and have put themselves outside the sphere of Islam." But terrorist attacks have continued. On July 7, 2005, in London, three bombs were detonated on subways and one on a bus, resulting in 52 deaths and hundreds of injuries. Saudi Arabia's chief legal authority immediately condemned the attacks. Less than two weeks later, the British Muslim Forum issued a fatwa signed by more than 500 British Muslim authorities, claiming, "Such acts ... are crimes against all of humanity and contrary to the teachings of Islam."

Sharia law, warfare, and human rights

Condemnations of terrorism have become routine following attacks; they are issued in traditional press releases and social media, and are readily accessible online.[5] Sustained arguments against terrorist interpretations of Islam are also available online. Among the most detailed is a 25-page point-by-point refutation of the claims made by Islamic State, signed by dozens of Sunni Muslim religious authorities and issued publicly in September 2014. Known as the "Open Letter to [IS leader] al-Baghdadi," it is a model of classical Sharia reasoning. Providing extensive background based on the Qur'an, the example of Prophet Muhammad (the Sunna, which is conveyed in reports called Hadith), and the opinions of the most widely recognized Sharia authorities throughout history, the letter demonstrates that Islam forbids the killing of innocent people. The classical protection of "emissaries, ambassadors, and diplomats" is extended in the modern categories of journalists and aid workers. The document amply demonstrates Islam's classical definition of jihad as defensive war. "It is not permissible without the right cause, the right purpose and without the right rules of conduct." The Letter to al-Baghdadi reiterates the prohibition of killing people based on their religious identity, and demonstrates that Islamic law prohibits waging war on people who have not attacked Muslims, evicted them from their homes, or prohibited them from practicing their religion. The letter acknowledges that a minority opinion allowing preemptive war ("offensive jihad") emerged in medieval Islam, but asserts that, even so, war cannot be based simply on differences of religion or opinion. Because of the atrocities committed by IS against followers of the ancient Mesopotamian Yazidi religion, the document specifically mentions Yazidis as protected in Islamic law, just as Jews and Christians are. In addition, the Letter to al-Baghdadi affirms that slavery has been outlawed in Islam by universal consensus (which is binding in Islamic jurisprudence), and so its reintroduction is forbidden. Forced conversion has always been prohibited in Islam, based on the Qur'an's direct statement that there can be no compulsion in religion (2:256). The sanctity of women's and children's lives, dignity, and property must be respected. Moreover, the document confirms that Islamic law forbids torture, the killing of prisoners, and the mutilation of corpses.

The Open Letter to al-Baghdadi also notes a key distinction between Qur'anic verses that pertain to the conduct of a war that has already begun, and verses that deal with peacetime. This is among the most confusing features of the Qur'an for people unfamiliar with both how scripture works and what is known as "just war theory." The Qur'an was delivered over more than 20 years in the early seventh century during a period of intense warfare among tribes – some Jewish, some Christian, many polytheistic. Its goal was to reassert the religion of Abraham, get the tribes to stop warring, and work for social justice. But of course some tribes rejected the efforts and launched battles against Muhammad and his followers. So while many verses talk about the importance of peace and working for justice, others talk about the importance of being valiant and not backing down during battle. That's why Qur'an interpreters are careful to identify the historical context before citing verses. If a verse deals with conduct during a battle, it can't be used to justify conduct during peacetime. But that's what the terrorists do. So the Open Letter to al-Baghdadi mentions a verse used by IS calling for harsh treatment of enemies, and points out that it is from a chapter of the Qur'an that was delivered during a battle, and therefore is not applicable outside that context. Indeed, there are dozens of verses that call for equitable treatment even of potential enemies during peacetime. Looking at the historical context of verses to understand their significance is a common method in scriptural interpretation. Who, for example, would think the Hebrew Bible's command to kill "men and women, children and infants, cattle and sheep, camels and donkeys" (1 Samuel 15:3) would apply outside of the time when it was delivered? Actually, the Qur'an's advice to fight ferociously in the midst of battle is very similar to that of Krishna described in the Hindu epic *Bhagavad Gita*. In both cases, the context was one of battles involving cousins fighting cousins – a major violation of tribal norms. In both cases, the wars were believed to be for a higher purpose, a just cause, and so the divine advice was to ignore the tribal norm and fight on. But the advice applied only during war, not outside of it. Outside of warfare, people are required to behave with fairness and civility. Unfortunately, non-specialists looking at the Qur'an sometimes mistake this specialized advice for general advice, as do the terrorists. So the religious authorities who produced the Open Letter to al-Baghdadi straighten them out. "As for God's words, '… and be harsh with them …' (9:73); and: '… and let them find harshness in you…' (9:123), this is during war, not after it."[6]

Three other issues covered in the Letter to al-Baghdadi deserve special attention because of the widespread misunderstanding of them by both the general public and Islamic terrorists. One concerns the physical punishments for crimes such as theft and adultery – the *hudud* punishments – specified in classical Islamic legal sources. The Qur'an places such strong emphasis on the right to private ownership of property, for example, that it calls for amputation of the hand of the thief (5:38). And it places such a strong value on the family that it specifies 100 lashes for adultery (24:2). (The punishment was later changed to capital punishment for adultery between two people married to other people, as in the Hebrew Bible [Leviticus 20:10].) However, the Letter to al-Baghdadi reminds readers that *hudud* punishments may only be implemented under special circumstances. The punishment for theft, for example, cannot be applied in cases of hunger, or for trivial amounts. *Hudud* punishments may only be implemented for sane, sober, and otherwise upstanding adults who willfully violate the law, and even then only with the strictest rules of evidence. Successful sentencing of capital punishment for adultery requires four adult, demonstrably honorable witnesses to the actual sexual act. If allegations of adultery are made and these rules of evidence cannot be met, the Qur'an specifies 80 lashes for the accuser (24:4).

Second, the whole idea of unilaterally declaring a caliphate – a single leader for all Muslims worldwide – is unfounded. The caliphate is a political institution established after the death of Muhammad in the seventh century. For a brief period – perhaps a few centuries – there really was political unity among Muslims. But the caliphate gradually became symbolic, as various regions achieved political autonomy. The basis of unity among Muslims was, as it remains, shared commitment to monotheistic beliefs and values of justice and human dignity as revealed by all prophets and epitomized in the revelations of the Qur'an. The position of caliphate survived until the end of World War I, when the last holders of the title – the Ottomans – were defeated. In 1924, the position was abolished. The Letter to al-Baghdadi confirms that Muslims share the ideal of a strong and unified community symbolized by the caliphate. But it also confirms that no one can just declare himself caliph and set about forcing everyone to accept it. The caliphate can only be reestablished by consensus among Muslims worldwide. Since Muslims comprise over one-fifth of the world's population, living in wildly divergent circumstances, including both the poorest and the richest people on earth, it will obviously be some time before that kind of consensus can be achieved, if ever. So the Letter points out that al-Baghdadi actually has no legitimacy as caliph. That's why the religious authorities in Mosul, Iraq – where he first declared himself caliph – rejected his claim. The killing of those authorities by the self-declared Islamic State is a perfect example of why people aren't allowed to impose their beliefs by force, say the religious authorities. All it does is create chaos, which undermines the stability and security Islam seeks to establish. The authorities then point out how preposterous it is for IS to appoint itself ruler of over a billion and a half Muslims and then declare all those who reject the claim – 99%, according to the Letter – as non-Muslims.

The third critical issue concerns mainstream Islamic notions of citizenship responsibilities. Related to al-Baghdadi's claim to be the only legitimate ruler of all Muslims worldwide is his group's demand that "true" Muslims abandon where they live and move to the territory they've claimed in Syria and Iraq. The term they use for this is *hijrah* – emigration. They claim that it is illegal for Muslims to live anywhere that isn't ruled by their unique version of Islamic law. This claim has convinced some Muslims to pack up and go to Syria or Iraq to join IS. The authorities point out that what IS is doing is actually illegally confiscating other people's property. To drive the point home, they compare its actions to those of Israelis occupying Palestinian territory. The Letter also points out that IS is wrong when it denounces patriotism and allegiance to the laws of one's country. It confirms that love of country is both natural and consistent with Islam. Other scholars have confirmed that loyalty to country is a religious duty in Islam. That includes the responsibility of Muslim members of the armed forces to serve loyally even in wars conducted in Muslim-majority countries.

There is no denying that the global terrorists – al-Qaeda and its even more radical spinoff, Islamic State – are fearsome, as are their wannabes such as Nigeria's Boko Haram and Somalia's al-Shabaab. They are terrorizing people not only in the West, but throughout the Middle East, South Asia, and beyond. But nor is there any denying that the vast majority of Muslims condemn their actions as violations of Islamic norms. They reject the claim that Islam is the source of terrorism. Legal scholar Cherif Bassiouni summarizes the mainstream position, saying that terrorists' violence may be in the name of Islam but it is not permitted in Islam.[7]

But if religion isn't the source of terrorists' actions, then what is? What is it that motivates the terrorists? The answer can be found in some of the same statements that condemn their actions. After the 2005 bombings in London, for example, British Muslim scholar Abd al-Hakim Murad called the attacks a "deep subversion" of Islamic law and a sign of profound decadence. He described the motivation of the terrorists as "rage, that desire to self-annihilation, to lash out," and their actions as "wild expression of futility and despair and vindictiveness."[8] But what are the rage and despair about? Murad mentioned just a few of their grievances: Israeli occupation of Palestinian territories, Russian control of Chechnya, and Indian control of Kashmir. Actually, these and other political issues are of profound concern to mainstream Muslims, too, but they deal with them in different ways. In the next two chapters we'll discuss these shared concerns, and how mainstream Muslims' means of dealing with them differ from those of global terrorists.

4

Shared Grievances

On September 20, 2001, US President George W. Bush addressed the nation regarding the events that had occurred in New York, Washington DC, and Somerset County, Pennsylvania, just nine days earlier. Before offering his answer, he proudly extolled Americans' shows of patriotic emotion in the wake of the atrocities: "the unfurling of flags, the lighting of candles, the giving of blood, the saying of prayers in English, Hebrew and Arabic." The president proceeded to valorize the shift from grief to anger and resolution to "bring our enemies to justice or bring justice to our enemies." One way or another, he said ominously, "Justice will be done." Then he raised a question. Americans wanted to know, he said: Why do "they" hate us? His answer: "They hate our freedoms: our freedom of religion, our freedom of speech, our freedom to vote and assemble and disagree with each other."[1]

Actually, religious freedom and other civil liberties had nothing to do with it. Al-Qaeda founder Osama bin Laden made it perfectly clear why he had ordered the attacks. His campaign against the West was announced in his 1996 "Declaration of War against the Americans Occupying the Land of the Two Holy Places." He was horrified that the Saudi ruling family had allowed the US military to defend its sacred soil rather than his own crack team of seasoned Mujahideen. But that indignity was only the last straw; there were many other grievances, and Bin Laden proceeded to itemize them as soon as he got through the pious praise of the Almighty and reminders that Scripture calls on believers to fight oppression. His inventory of the injustices suffered by Muslims since the Europeans took control of the Muslim world during the colonial era included Palestine, Iraq, Lebanon, Somalia, Bosnia, Chechnya, Burma, Kashmir, the Philippines, Eritrea, Assam, Pattani, and Ogaden. This list demonstrated, said Bin Laden, that Muslims' blood had become the cheapest in the world and their natural resources "loot in the hands of the enemies." A year after the 9/11 attacks, he issued a follow-up "Letter to America." Acknowledging Mr Bush's question, he asked, "Why have we attacked you? Because you attacked us and continue to attack us."[2] He then offered a slightly different list of grievances. Palestine and Iraq again topped the list, but this time some of the more obscure references were excluded, replaced by US support for authoritarian governments in the Middle East, and Afghanistan – which the United States had invaded a month after the 9/11 attacks.

Bin Laden's messages were widely disseminated (and are still available online). But apparently Mr Bush and many others failed to read them. Those who read beyond the headlines know that the overwhelming majority of Muslims condemn terrorism, but they also know that many share some of the same concerns trotted out in terrorist manifestos. As noted in chapter 3, just two days after 9/11, Yusuf al-Qaradawi, Sunni Islam's most popular preacher, called the attacks "a grave sin." This, despite his strong opposition to many aspects of US foreign policy. The same attitude was also expressed by Rached Ghannouchi, leader of Tunisia's leading Islamist party, al-Nahda, and Iran's Supreme Leader Ayatollah Ali Khamenei.[3] Yet many people remain unaware of the post-colonial conditions against which both the majority of Muslims struggle peacefully on a daily basis, and radical terrorists explode in rage. Indeed, many Muslims are aware of that ignorance, which only adds insult to injury. Media critic John Powers reported that right after 9/11, CNN aired footage of a demonstration in Pakistan's capital city of Islamabad. A group of students carried a banner, written in English for the international press. It read: "America, think about why you are hated the world over." Powers concluded, "They hate us because we don't even know why they hate us."[4] So in order to comprehend the complex relationship between Muslims and the West, it is important to understand some of their major concerns.

Palestine: paradigm of post-colonial injustice

The most commonly recognized and longest-running grievance of Muslims worldwide is the statelessness of Palestinians. Palestine is a heritage that Islam shares with its monotheistic siblings Judaism and Christianity, and its story is well known throughout the Muslim world. The land referred to as Palestine was controlled by the Romans at the time of Jesus. Jewish rebellions against Roman rule in the first and second centuries led to their expulsion, leaving only a minority of Jews in the area. Islam arose in the region in the seventh century, and one of its first military victories was the defeat of the Romans. Palestine remained under the sovereignty of Muslims until the defeat of the Ottoman Empire in World War I. Under Islamic law, Jews and Christians were guaranteed religious freedom. Many converted to Islam, but Jews and Christians remained vital minorities in Palestine.

Prior to World War I, various European powers had made inroads into Ottoman lands. France, Britain, Spain, and Italy had gained control of significant portions of North Africa and the Middle East as the Ottoman Empire receded into its base: the modern country of Turkey. The Arabs of North Africa and the Middle East – Muslims, Christians, and Jews alike – were not happy that the Turks were letting this happen. The Europeans were not in the region for the well-being of the Arabs; they were there for their own economic benefit. And Europe's profit was Arabs' loss. As for the Ottomans, who had been far stronger than European powers throughout the Middle Ages, they had noticed that their traditional ways were no longer competitive. So in the early twentieth century they had undertaken modernization programs, with European assistance – in the case of the military, this came largely from Germany, which at the time was on a collision course with Britain, France, and Russia.

Consequently, when war exploded in 1914, the Turks were there to help Germany. With their assistance, it inflicted a devastating defeat on Britain at Gallipoli in 1915–16. The Allies decided they needed to prevent Germany from getting any further assistance from its Turkish protégés. Aware that the Arabs were restive under Turkish control, the British offered the Arabs independence if they would rebel against the Turks. That they did, which kept the Turks occupied until the defeat of the Central Powers in 1918. But the European Allies broke their promises to the Arabs. Instead of recognizing Arab independence, they divided Arab lands among themselves, in accordance with a secret agreement they had signed in 1916. This "Sykes–Picot Agreement" gave French control over the parts of traditional Syria now known as Syria and Lebanon. And it gave the British control over what is now known as Iraq, as well as those portions of traditional Syria known as Palestine and the modern country of Jordan. The agreement is largely forgotten in the West, but it is front and center in jihadi literature. Poets condemn it, IS leader al-Baghdadi vows to undo it, and the two-minute section dealing with it in the 1962 Hollywood blockbuster *Lawrence of Arabia* is all over social media.

The story of European betrayal of promises made to Arabs sounds like ancient history to many people in the West. But not to Jews, because of what happened next. British Palestine was declared a home for European Jews desperate to escape the horrors of anti-Semitism. Britain issued a declaration in 1917 recognizing Palestine as a homeland for the world's Jews and pledging to "use their best endeavours to facilitate the achievement of this object." This "Balfour Declaration" was then included in the agreements establishing British control over Palestine.

The initial response of Arabs was acceptance of Jewish immigration into Palestine, provided the promised independent Arab state became a reality. But that didn't happen. The traditional leaders in the Arabian peninsula who had agreed to assist the British in World War I in return for Arab independence, the Hashemites, were defeated by a tribal confederation from central Arabia, the Saudis, in 1925. The Saudis then took over most of the Arabian peninsula and named it after themselves. Feisal bin Hussein bin Ali, one of the deposed Hashemite leaders, was given the title of king in Syria, under French control. When he and the

Syrians rebelled against French control, however, they were defeated and the king was ousted. He was then given the title of king in Iraq, under British control. His brother Abdullah was made king in Jordan, under British tutelage. Palestine remained under direct British control. At the same time, European anti-Semitism was escalating to horrific levels, creating a huge refugee crisis and increased immigration into Palestine. At the time of the Balfour Declaration, Jews constituted about 11% of Palestine's population. Within a decade, that percentage had doubled due to European immigration, and that alarmed local inhabitants.

The late 1930s were marked by Arab uprisings against British control of Palestine. Meanwhile, rising Nazism in Europe led to exponentially increased Jewish immigration into the territory. British efforts to limit this immigration led to Jewish attacks on British administrators. Inevitably, immigrant and local Jews were pitted against local Muslims and Christians. Europe's Jews were fighting for their very survival; Palestinian Muslims and Christians were fighting for their land.

Back in Europe, exhausted by its struggle against the Nazis in World War II, Britain could no longer afford to maintain control in Palestine. In 1947, it therefore gave the problem over to the newly created

United Nations, which voted to partition the region into two states – one for Jews, regardless of their country of origin, and one for Arabs, regardless of their religious identity. Six months later, in May 1948, the League of Nations-mandated British control of Palestine expired, and Israel declared itself a sovereign country. The Arab countries, including those still under British control, immediately declared war – and lost. After that first Arab–Israeli war, Israel had gained a significant amount of territory beyond that designated for a Jewish state by the United Nations, Jordan took control of the area designated as a Palestinian state on the West Bank of the Jordan River, Egypt took effective control of the Palestinian territory known as the Gaza Strip, and nearly 800,000 Palestinians became refugees. They took refuge in UN-run camps in the West Bank, Gaza, and neighboring countries. Almost 70 years later, those camps still exist.

Egypt achieved independence from Britain in 1952. Its leader, Colonel Gamal Abdul Nasser, threatened to take back Palestinian land from Israel, prompting Israel to invade Egypt in 1967. Syria and Jordan came to Egypt's assistance, but again the Arabs were defeated. Israel took control of the West Bank and Gaza Strip, creating another wave of refugees. Another Arab effort to regain Palestinian territory in 1973 led to yet another defeat. Today the number of Palestinian refugees registered with the United Nations Relief and Works Agency (UNRWA) is nearly 5 million.[5]

Following the 1967 and 1973 Arab–Israeli wars, the UN Security Council called for Israel to withdraw from the Palestinian territories of the West Bank and Gaza Strip, citing the illegality of occupying territory by force. Israel did not comply. Instead it established colonial settlements in both areas. In 2005, it dismantled the settlements in Gaza, but to this day it maintains strict control of the territory's borders, including intrusive buffer zones and strict import restrictions. Gazan fighters have launched periodic rocket attacks on Israel in an effort to break its control, but these have led to two punishing wars that have only intensified its hold. Repeated UN calls for Israeli withdrawal from the territories occupied in 1967 have been fruitless, as have non-violent resistance movements. The West Bank and East Jerusalem remain under Israeli military occupation, hosting some half million Israelis in illegal settlements established by the government of Israel. Despite limited autonomy in Gaza and the West Bank, Palestinians remain stateless.

Gaza is one of the poorest places on earth, its water sources contaminated and infrastructure demolished by Israeli airstrikes. Life in the West Bank is only slightly better. Violation of Palestinian rights has been well documented since the beginning of Israel's occupation of the West Bank and Gaza. Each war has brought a spike in offenses and accusations of war crimes, most recently the summer 2014 50-day Gaza War. Amnesty International reports that during that conflict Israeli forces killed more than 1,500 civilians including 539 children, and wounded thousands more. In addition to "massive civilian displacement and destruction of property and vital services," the report continues:

> Israel maintained its air, sea and land blockade of Gaza, imposing collective punishment on its approximately 1.8 million inhabitants and stoking the humanitarian crisis. In the West Bank, Israeli forces carried out unlawful killings of Palestinian protesters, including children, and maintained an array of oppressive restrictions on Palestinians' freedom of movement while continuing to promote illegal settlements and allow Israeli settlers to attack Palestinians and destroy their property with near total impunity. Israeli forces detained thousands of Palestinians, some of whom reported being tortured, and held around 500 administrative detainees without trial. Within Israel, the authorities continued to demolish homes of Palestinian

> Bedouin in "unrecognized villages" ... and commit forcible evictions. They also detained and summarily expelled thousands of foreign migrants, including asylum-seekers, and imprisoned Israeli conscientious objectors.[6]

Other grievances

There are many other grievances shared by mainstream Muslims and global jihadis. Like the Palestine–Israel conflict, they can be traced to the end of empires and manipulation of subjugated peoples by European powers. The unresolved status of Kashmir in the northwest of the Indian subcontinent is a prominent example. Britain ruled India indirectly from the eighteenth century through the end of World War II. And as in Palestine following World War II, Britain decided to partition the lands it could no longer control. In this case, the partition designated certain lands for Hindus and others for Muslims. The 1947 Partition of India is what led to the creation of Pakistan and Bangladesh. But Kashmir – a beautiful region high in the Himalayas – created a problem for the partitioners. Its population was predominantly Muslim, but its ruler was a Hindu. Competing claims by India, Pakistan, and those who want an independent Kashmir have led to three wars between India and Pakistan and countless thousands of casualties. Claims of human rights abuses by India are widespread. The region remains divided between India and Pakistan at an uneasy and heavily militarized "Line of Control."

Bin Laden's 1996 message also mentioned Somalia – familiar to Americans since the hit 2001 film *Black Hawk Down*. Located on the Horn of Africa, bordered by the Red Sea and Indian Ocean, Somalia has the longest shoreline and some of the most beautiful beaches in Africa. The region was a highly profitable trade center from ancient times. It was so valuable that Britain and Italy competed for it, brutally suppressing local resistance movements. Eventually they divided it into British Somaliland and Italian Somaliland. In 1941, Britain gained full control, and then in 1960 it granted independence to the country. But the two regions – the former Italian Somaliland in the south and the former British Somaliland in the north – had little in common, not even languages. Their politics were clan based, laying the groundwork for competition in the newly united country. What is more, the British and Italians had established the country's borders in a way that left large minorities of Somalis in neighboring Kenya and Ethiopia –

another recipe for unrest. Unrest led to instability, resulting in a military coup in 1969. In 1977, the military government sparked a war with Ethiopia when it tried to incorporate that country's ethnic Somali region – Ogaden – into Somalia. After initial success, Somalia was forced to retreat from Ethiopia due to Soviet military intervention. The Somali government thus became a staunch US ally in the Cold War. But its authoritarian ways led to the outbreak of civil war in the late 1980s. The central government was overthrown and the country receded into competing clan-based local governments. As these groups compete, backed by diverse external powers, the population suffers from lack of even the most basic human needs. In 1991, then UN Secretary-General Boutros Boutros-Ghali described the situation as "genocide by starvation." Successive droughts have only made the situation worse for Somalis, as the civil war continues.[7] Hundreds of thousands have become refugees. Others have turned to "parallel economies" like piracy and militias, including the infamous al-Shabaab, who have recently sworn allegiance to Islamic State. Again, the poverty and chaos are seen as results of Western imperialism.

Chechnya is another trouble spot mentioned by Bin Laden. At the time of his 1996 message, most

Westerners had never heard of it. But like Somalia, Chechnya began to register in the Western attention zone following terrorist attacks. The 2013 Boston Marathon bombing burned the name into Western consciousness. Three spectators were killed and over 250 more were wounded. The perpetrators, Tamerlan and Djokhar Tsarnaev, represented no terrorist organization, but they were outraged by the treatment of Chechnyans by Russia. Chechnya is a small region situated in the mountainous region between the Black and Caspian seas. Like Afghanistan, it was important historically because of its location on the world's major ancient trade route: the Silk Road. Therefore, it was attacked by every would-be emperor who came along. The Russians began trying to gain control of the region in the sixteenth century under Ivan the Terrible, whose Russian name – Ivan Grozny – gave Chechnya's capital its name. Chechnya found protection under Persia, but Russia's expansionist Peter the Great defeated the Persians in the early eighteenth century. Chechen and other tribes fiercely resisted the Russians in countless battles even after Russia was ultimately able to dominate the region in the early nineteenth century. When the Communist Bolsheviks overthrew the Romanov tsars in 1917, Chechnya (and its neighboring Ingushetia and

Dagestan) declared independence. But the Soviets retook the region in 1921.

The horrors endured by Chechens and others under Russians and Soviets are almost indescribable. During World War II, for example, the Soviets falsely accused them of supporting the Nazi German invaders and forced most of them to relocate to Siberia and other frigid regions in mid-winter. Those who resisted were shot. The Boston Marathon bombers' family were among the deportees. The forced population transfer resulted in untold suffering, including the deaths of more than half the population. It was condemned as a genocide in 2004 by the European Parliament.

When the Soviet Union disbanded in 1991, Chechens again declared themselves independent. But again Russia would not allow it. In 1994, Russia unleashed a punishing military campaign. Chechnya's elected leader, Drozkhar Dudayev, was assassinated two years later and, as in Somalia, chaos reigned supreme. Profiteers and armed gangs, including self-declared Islamists, tried to exploit the situation for their own gain. Some launched terror attacks within Russia, killing hundreds of civilians. This led to brutal reprisals and another war with Russia. By spring 2000, after tens of thousands of deaths, largely civilian, the war was officially over.

But the insurgency continues, as do reports of horrific human rights violations. Russian journalist and human rights activist Anna Politskovskaya, an outspoken critic of Russian leader Vladimir Putin who led the onslaught against Chechnya, reported on extensive persecution of Chechens and others in books such as *A Dirty War* (2001) and *A Small Corner of Hell* (2003). She was assassinated in 2006.

Bin Laden mentioned other places, too, including Bosnia, where over 8,000 Muslim civilians were massacred during the war following the breakup of Yugoslavia. And Burma, where Nobel Peace Prize winner and now State Counsellor Aung San Suu Kyi has been criticized for her silence on her country's discrimination against the Rohingya Muslims. Human Rights Watch reports systematic repression of this community, including denial of citizenship, restrictions on religion, employment, and freedom of movement, and forced relocations. Over 140,000 were forced out of their homes in 2012 alone due to violence.[8]

These and similar post-colonial conflicts matter to Muslims worldwide, as they do to all people concerned with global human rights, peace, and security. But the majority of Muslims reject the global jihadi agenda and strategies. Even Islamist groups that have used terrorist tactics to resist occupation, such as Palestine's Hamas, have no global anti-West agenda. Their concerns are strictly nationalist. A recent report from a Palestinian policy organization decrying global jihadis' exploitation of the Palestinian cause is instructive. It points out that IS criticizes Palestinian leaders more than it criticizes Israel and actively tries to exploit Palestinian suffering to swell its ranks. The report confirms the nationalist objective of all Palestinian movements. "[E]ven within groups such as Hamas, the predominant identity is a Palestinian rather than a Muslim one, and the political goal is Palestinian self-determination, not the establishment of a transnational Islamic state." That explains why 88% of Palestinians denounce IS and 77% support Western and Arab attacks on IS.[9]

So, yes, Muslims worldwide share many concerns. But most have no interest in a global Islamic state. Even those who use terrorist tactics do so in the limited contexts of nationalist agendas. And in fact, instead of terrorist attacks against the presumed "masters of the universe" ("the West"), the majority of Muslims work peacefully within their own communities to advance their goals of good governance and development. That is the subject of the next chapter.

5

Mainstream Muslim Strategies

The grievances just described have their roots in European colonialism, something experienced by most Muslim-majority countries. This chapter examines how Muslims generally deal with the resulting challenges, focusing on socioeconomic and political development, and often maintaining strong relationships with the West, despite concerns over the impact of Western policies on their populations.

The largest Muslim population is in Indonesia – over 250 million people, 88% Muslim, comprising over 13% of the world's Muslims. After that comes Pakistan. In fact, nearly one-third of the world's Muslims live in Asia. Like all formerly colonized people, they aspire toward development, democracy, and human rights. And, despite the challenges resulting from their colonial heritage, by and large they maintain positive relations with the West.

Asia

Indonesia emerged as an independent country after a bloody struggle to evict a European colonial power, the Netherlands, in 1949. Exceedingly diverse ethnically and linguistically, thanks to borders that were imposed to suit colonial powers rather than local preferences, the country was potentially unstable. It was dominated by the military from the outset, but its first leader, General Sukarno, established democracy as the country's ultimate goal. He established the famous "five principles" – Pancasila – that have guided the country's democratic development since independence: Indonesian nationalism, international standards of justice, democratic governance, social well-being, and monotheism. The army organized Indonesia's first elections to establish a national legislature in 1955, but ethnic and ideological rivalries plagued the country. In an effort to quell unrest, Sukarno's government reduced the power of parliament and limited civil liberties. These measures led to popular discontent and a military coup. The coup was followed by a violent backlash against Communists, who were blamed for the discontent, as well as anyone suspected of being a leftist. In 1967, staunchly pro-West Major General Suharto took charge, confirmed by elections in the following year.

The military reinstated limited democracy but there were still problems. One of the country's 14,000 islands, Timor, had been divided by the Netherlands and Portugal in 1914. When the Netherlands gave up its colonies, only West Timor became part of Indonesia. East Timor remained under Portuguese control until Portugal departed in 1975. Indonesia then annexed East Timor, but the East Timorese were adamantly opposed to the annexation. Indonesia's military led a violent campaign to bring East Timor to heel, leading to an estimated 200,000 deaths and horrific human rights violations. In addition, there was continued discontent among Indonesians calling for greater democratic reforms and accusations of corruption circulated widely. The Asian financial crisis of 1997 and the collapse of Indonesia's currency led to massive protests that ultimately brought Suharto down.

Throughout his tenure, Suharto remained a solid Western ally, given his anti-Communist stance. But he couldn't suppress Indonesians' demands for democracy.

With the ouster of Suharto, Indonesians finally got the chance to choose their president. In 1999, they elected Abdurrahman Wahid, the leader of the country's pro-democracy Muslim organization, Nahdlatul Ulama. Gus Dur, as he was popularly known, was beloved and highly respected for restoring civil and political rights, curbing corruption, and improving ethnic relations, especially with Indonesia's Chinese minority. And he received high praise for firing the general who oversaw the East Timor atrocities, apologizing to the people of East Timor, and setting up a tribunal to examine human rights abuses there. But his administrative skills were non-existent and so parliament replaced him with his vice-president, Sukarno's daughter, Megawati Sukarnoputri.

Soon after Sukarnoputri's election, the world was introduced to al-Qaeda through the 9/11 attacks. Al-Qaeda-linked terrorists attacked in Indonesia, too, killing over 200 people in a Bali nightclub bombing in 2002. Police investigations led to four convictions. There have been several other similar attacks in Indonesia against targets considered symbolic of the West, and Indonesian authorities have continued to cooperate with the West in counter-terrorism.

Sukarnoputri was defeated in 2004 elections by Susilo Bambang Yudhoyono, from the Indonesian Democratic Party (PDI). SBY, as he is popularly known, oversaw economic recovery and improvement of civilian infrastructure, including healthcare and education. Those measures, combined with his championing of environmental causes, earned him reelection in 2009. The 2014 elections brought victory for Joko Widodo, known as Jokowi. Faced with economic challenges, Jokowi has yet to prove himself, but Muslim Indonesia's democracy is alive and well, and the country remains a Western ally. Its Malacca Strait, linking the Indian Ocean and the Pacific Rim, is one the most important shipping lanes in the world. It is therefore vital to Western economic interests. Indonesia cooperates with Western powers to maintain its security and continues to cooperate in counter-terrorism. And despite the unpopularity of some Western policies, public opinion polls show that some two-thirds of Indonesians view the United States favorably.[1]

Pakistan, with around 185 million people, is, as noted above, the second largest Muslim-majority country. It was established as a homeland for the subcontinent's Muslims when Britain left India in 1947. According to its Objectives Resolution, passed in 1948, Pakistan was to be a democratic state whose power is exercised "through the chosen representatives of the people." It would be based on Islamic principles, articulated as "democracy, freedom, equality, tolerance and social justice," and an independent judiciary.

But Pakistan has not had an easy path toward

fulfilling its democratic goals. To begin with, it was carved out of India and left with no functioning bureaucracy other than the military. What's more, the original country comprised East Pakistan and West Pakistan, divided by over 1,000 miles of hostile territory, as well as languages and cultures. Power-sharing in such a situation proved impossible, leading to civil war and the establishment of Bangladesh – formerly East Pakistan – in 1971. In addition, its border dispute with India over Kashmir has led to three wars, and remains unresolved. Moreover, neighboring Afghanistan was occupied by the USSR during the 1980s, landing Pakistan in the position of surrogate to the United States, in its campaign against its Soviet archenemy. The result of these factors is that the military has dominated Pakistan's brief history. Its civilian governments have been ousted in military coups three times – on each occasion with Western support.

Furthermore, military establishments are expensive. Military expenditures account for the largest single share of Pakistan's national budget, and corruption among Pakistan's ruling elites is rampant. Prime ministers have been dismissed from office on allegations or actual charges of corruption at least three times. This is only one indicator of the country's culture of corruption, which has left it economically stagnant. In 2014, the dismal state of social services, including healthcare and education, earned Pakistan the rank of 147th (of 188 measured) by the UN Human Development Index – compiling data regarding life expectancy, education, and per capita income.[2]

Economic stresses inevitably lead to social unrest, especially in diverse countries where economic disadvantage can be perceived in ethnic terms. Pakistan has always been dominated by elites from its two eastern provinces, Punjab and Sindh. That has left western provinces feeling marginalized. Baluchistan, bordering Iran, is Pakistan's largest. Its natural gas fields, copper and gold resources, and its long coastline and accessible ports on the Indian Ocean make it one of the country's most valuable provinces. But it feels underrepresented nationally. The province to its north, Khyber Pakhtun-Khwa, formerly the Northwest Frontier Province, is also called Afghania – the home of the Afghans, otherwise known as Pashtuns (and Pathans and Pakhtuns). But Pakistan's Pashtuns account for only about two-thirds of that people's world population. The other third are in Afghanistan, as a result of another inept partition of other people's land by Britain. That was in 1893. The "Durand Line," running some 1,500 miles over some of the world's highest mountains, marked the extent of Britain's sovereignty in India. But the border remains porous to the skilled Afghan mountaineers who call it home. It is relatively easy for those resisting US dominance in Afghanistan to take refuge among their co-tribesmen in Pakistan. That's why the United States began its drone warfare in Pakistan in 2004. Notoriously imprecise, that campaign has led to – literally – countless civilian deaths in Pakistan, fueling anti-American sentiment. Indeed, the US drone attacks in Pakistan have proven an effective recruiting tool for Pakistan's radicals. Among the results has been the targeting of Pakistan's Christian minority as a symbol of the West, as in the Lahore suicide bombings in March 2016, which killed over 70 people.

But Pakistan's democratic core has continued to function. Military governments have repeatedly been replaced by democratic governance due to public pressure. Most recently, the military rule of US-ally General Pervez Musharraf was ousted in 2008. And younger generations of voters have increasingly supported Pakistan's first successful new political party since the 1970s. The Pakistan Movement for Justice (*Pakistan Tehreek-e-Insaf*) was founded in 1996 by philanthropist (and former cricketer) Imran Khan. A rock star among Pakistan's politically engaged youth, Imran Khan champions democracy, development of civilian infrastructure, and an end to corruption and collaboration in foreign wars – all described in terms of core Islamic values. Moreover, despite the unpopularity of Western policies in the region, Pakistan remains a strategic ally of the West in counter-terrorism. Trade relations also remain strong: the United States and the European Union are Pakistan's largest trade partners.

The third largest Muslim population is in India, although here they comprise a distinct minority (around 15%). Lingering resentments from the violence surrounding the 1947 partition of India have flared into open hostilities on occasion. Riots erupted in Bombay (Mumbai) in the winter of 1992–3, killing 900, after the demolition of the Babri Masjid, a sixteenth-century mosque. In 2002, sectarian violence again exploded in Gujarat, each side accusing the other of radicalism. Brutality against civilians, including women and children, marked the Gujarat riots, resulting in thousands of deaths, mostly of Muslims. The hostilities have been blamed variously on escalating Hindu nationalism and Islamic radicalism, represented by the Mumbai terror attacks of 1993, 2006, and 2008. Nevertheless, Muslims continue to participate in India's thriving democracy. They are well represented in Indian business and culture, including the ever-popular Bollywood. Three of India's 12 presidents have been Muslim; four have held the office of chief justice.

Bangladesh, the former East Pakistan, is the fourth largest Muslim-majority country. In precolonial times it had been among India's richest regions, but colonial policies left it one of the poorest. The 1971 civil war that led to the creation of Bangladesh devastated the country further. The West Pakistan army destroyed civilian infrastructure, businesses, homes, and agricultural resources. After the creation of Bangladesh, famine struck again. The 1974 famine, resulting from floods and inept government policies, claimed up to a million victims. The following year saw two military coups. Four years later, Lieutenant General Ziaur Rahman restored civilian rule. The country's founding Awami League party had placed Bangladesh on a socialist course. Rahman founded the Bangladesh Nationalist Party (BNP) and attempted to reorient the country toward capitalism. But he also faced coups and ethnic unrest and was assassinated by a military faction in 1981. Democracy was finally restored in 1991 and Rahman's widow, Khaleda Zia, became prime minister. Elections in 1996 brought the founding Awami League back to power.

Its leader, Sheikh Hasina, stabilized the country, negotiating cooperation with India, Pakistan, and Turkey. But economic challenges continued. In 2001, elections brought BNP leader Khaleda Zia back at the head of an alliance. Efforts to strengthen the country's economy, social services, and international relations continued. But Zia's government faced corruption charges, leading to the imposition of a caretaker government in 2006. Popular discontent and protests against the government prompted the military to declare a state of emergency, but 2008 saw the return to democracy once again with Sheikh Hasina of the Awami League restored as prime minister – a post she retained in the 2014 elections. As in the case of Indonesia and Pakistan, throughout its turbulent history, Bangladesh has remained cooperative with Western countries in regional defense and counter-terrorism.

The Middle East

Middle Eastern countries – Turkish, Persian, and Arab – provide more examples of mainstream Muslim efforts to recover from the colonial era. Turkey, with about 75 million people, is one of the oldest democracies in the region. It emerged from the Ottoman Empire following World War I and the abolition of the caliphate. But already Turkey had a strong democratic heritage. In the 1870s, reformers successfully pressured the ruling "sultan" to establish a constitutional democracy. It existed in name only for some time, but by 1908 the government was forced to allow multiparty elections. After the war, modern Turkey's founding father, Mustafa Kemal "Atatürk," launched a new democracy and development projects. His goal was to establish a strong Turkey with a modern economy – in a hurry. That meant that many of his projects were managed from the top down, bypassing traditional religious authorities and often leaving the general public feeling disoriented.

Atatürk died on the eve of World War II, in which Turkey sided with the Western Allies. Like many people, Turks feared Communist expansion. Turkish troops fought against the Communists in the Korean War, and in 1952 Turkey joined NATO, the North Atlantic Treaty Organization, designed to protect the West from Communist expansion. Continued fears of Soviet expansion, border disputes, and ethnic tensions led to instability in Turkey, resulting in military coups in 1960, 1972, and 1980. But democracy has continued to be the government of choice in Turkey.

Leftists and right-wing militarists clashed during the 1970s, making that a particularly turbulent time for Turkey. Stability and democracy were restored in the 1980s, but discontent with the military-dominated traditional elites led to new democratic movements, including leftist and religiously oriented parties. Two parties espousing both democracy and religious values rose to prominence: the Welfare Party and the Motherland Party. Reflecting popular discontent with secular parties' performance, both parties found support in the 1995 elections.

Traditional secular elites felt threatened by this rising populism. The Welfare Party was banned in 1998, and so was its successor, the Virtue Party, in 2001. A new Islamist party emerged from the remnants of the Welfare Party, the Justice and Development Party, known by its Turkish initials as the AKP. The AKP dominated the 2002 parliamentary elections, running on a platform of pluralism, prosperity, and pragmatism. Significant improvements in Turkey's economy and social services have led to the party's continued popularity. The AKP and its leader, Recep Tayyip Erdoğan, have led Turkey's government ever since.

Erdoğan and the AKP are not without their detractors. The government's efforts to marginalize the military by strengthening the presidency have led to fears of rising authoritarianism. And the party's overt Islamism has alarmed diehard secularists. But the party has continued to win elections, and Turkey has remained a loyal Western ally. The US-led invasion of Iraq in 2003 and the resulting and ongoing war in Syria and general regional instability have cooled Turkish attitudes toward the West, and Turkey's alleged double-dealing with IS has cooled Western attitudes toward Turkey. But the country remains steadfastly in the Western camp. US and British forces have used Incirlik Air Base near the Syrian border since the 1950s; Incirlik, in fact, is a major NATO nuclear weapons storage site.

The other large non-Arab country in the Middle East is Iran. Like Turkey, the monarchy of Persia, as it was then called, was confronted with a constitutional revolution in the first decade of the twentieth century. As in Turkey, too, neighboring Russia was a threat. Russia had taken control of oil-rich areas north of the Caspian Sea, on Iran's northern border, during the nineteenth century. And the monarchy had sold off Persia's southern oil resources to what became British Petroleum (BP), in 1901. In 1907, Britain and Russia agreed to split the country into spheres of influence, sponsoring their own local militias. During World War I, Britain and Russia both moved into Persia to protect their interests. Following the war, Iran's military leaders took over. The leader of one of the foreign-backed brigades had himself crowned, becoming Reza Shah ("king") Pahlavi.

Like his hero Atatürk, Reza Shah tried to quickly modernize and strengthen his country. (He's the one who renamed Persia Iran, stressing the country's non-Arab identity: "Iran" means "Aryan," while Arabs are Semites.) He considered traditional religion an impediment and took measures to modernize it, including prohibiting traditional turbans and veils. The rapid modernization and social engineering had unsettling effects among the general public. When they organized political opposition, the Shah banned political parties, further alienating the public.

During World War II, Russia and Britain therefore again occupied the country. Distrusting Reza Shah, they forced him to abdicate in favor of his son, Muhammad Reza. The new Shah was very pro-West, but foreign control of the country's resources remained unpopular. Opposition to the Shah's policies became increasingly organized. A popular coalition in parliament demanded that the government negotiate for Iranian control of its own petroleum. In 1951, the Shah had to bow to popular pressure. The popular pro-nationalization prime minister Muhammad Mossadegh immediately set out to take back Iran's oil resources.

Naturally the British opposed the plan. They took measures to maintain their control, culminating in a joint undercover mission with the US to unseat Mosaddegh in 1953. He was arrested, sentenced to three years' solitary confinement, and then spent the rest of his life under house arrest. The Shah's power was reinforced, but although Iran received an increased share of profits, BP retained control of Iran's oil production, now in consortium with US and European companies.

But the Shah's government became more authoritarian, and more unpopular, as did his foreign backers. The Shah was able to silence political opposition, the press, academics, and artists, but he couldn't silence the voices of religious leaders. Even in exile, they became the default voice of popular opposition. And Operation Ajax – the code name for the overthrow of Mosaddegh (in the United States; it was called Operation Boot in the United Kingdom) – became the symbol of Western greed and duplicity.

That was the background for the 1979 Islamic Revolution in Iran and the exile of the Shah. When the United States allowed him to come to New York, that triggered the occupation of the US embassy in Tehran and the famous 444-day "hostage crisis." Opposition to the United States increased in the immediate aftermath of the revolution, when it supported Iraq's invasion of Iran.

The Iran–Iraq war stalled Iran's democratization yet again. But in 1997, Iranians elected a liberal reformer, Mohammad Khatami, by a landslide. President Khatami was a great advocate of intellectual freedom and openness to the West, and democracy. Younger generations loved this message, but it was hard to persuade the Old Guard that the West could be trusted. In 2001, al-Qaeda's 9/11 attacks and the subsequent US occupation of Iran's eastern neighbor Afghanistan allowed the Old Guard to claim they had been right. President Khatami was replaced by the deeply anti-West Mahmoud Ahmadinejad in 2005.

But Iran's reformers continued their efforts. Their calls for economic and political reform resonated widely in the run-up to presidential elections in 2009. When Ahmadinejad was declared the winner, people suspected fraud and massive protests erupted. Defying a ban on public demonstrations, Iranians staged an innovative protest. An estimated three million people filled the streets of Tehran, maintaining complete silence. Thus was born Iran's

Green Movement, which helped bring the reformist Hassan Rouhani to the presidency in 2013.

President Rouhani remains very popular in Iran, and that popularity allowed his government to negotiate an agreement with the West in 2015 designed to prohibit the country from developing nuclear weapons but allow it to develop nuclear power, and begin repairing relations with the West that were destroyed during the 1979 revolution. The old revolutionary elites remain suspicious, however, and they maintain ultimate control of the country's military and foreign policy. This is particularly evident in the context of ongoing wars in neighboring Iraq, Syria, and Yemen.

Egypt, the largest Arab country, with some 90 million people, held successful democratic elections after decades of military rule, in 2012. But, unfortunately, that progress was soon reversed, again due to regional geopolitical complications. Egypt was part of the British Empire until independence in the 1950s. As often happened, independence was gained through a military coup, which left the military in charge. That was true from 1952 until the overthrow of Hosni Mubarak as part of the "Arab Spring" in 2012. There had been a parliament and various forms of elections since the nineteenth century, but it was only in 2012 that elections deemed free and fair were held, and they resulted in the election of Muhammad Morsi, a representative of the oldest Islamist organization, the Muslim Brotherhood.

The Muslim Brotherhood is a mainstream organization that rejects violence – a stance that has earned the repeated condemnation of al-Qaeda and Islamic State leaders. The Brotherhood's focus for its nearly 90-year history has been providing social services such as education and healthcare. It considers these services a means of reforming and improving society in accordance with Islamic values – a counterbalance to Western consumerist values. These services have also fulfilled vital functions, since successive military-dominated governments have neglected them, focusing instead on increasing the wealth and power of the elites. As a result, the Brotherhood became widely popular among Egypt's majority non-elites. That accounts for their strong showing in Egypt's first ever democratic elections.

But the Brotherhood's focus on social services also accounts for its inexperience in governing. Morsi himself is a physician with no governing experience. The group admittedly made serious errors in its first go at governance, including forming a coalition with an ultra-conservative Islamist group. But of more concern to the elites was the

Brotherhood's populist democracy. What would happen to their control of national resources? The idea of dissipating concentrated wealth among the masses worried not just Egyptian elites but also the region's oil-rich monarchies. They supported counter-revolutionary forces promulgating claims that the Muslim Brotherhood was a front for al-Qaeda, orchestrating economic slowdowns in Egypt, and empowering Egypt's military to stage a coup within a year of Morsi's election.

Since summer 2013, Egypt has been under the watchful eye of Africa's strongest military. The coup was confirmed in a sham election in 2014. (Field Marshal Abd al-Fattah al-Sisi, the leader of the coup, won with over 96% of the votes cast.) Government forces had killed nearly 1,000 pro-democracy demonstrators in the infamous Rabaa Square massacre of August 2013, and since then over 40,000 have been taken political prisoner, including journalists and students. The government has staged sham mass trials, as well, condemning hundreds to death – many *in absentia*. Also condemned to death are the country's democratically elected president and most leaders of the Muslim Brotherhood, human rights activists and journalists, as well as the leading Sunni Muslim preacher Yusuf al-Qaradawi, a vocal opponent of terrorism.

So Egypt is once more – as the saying goes – not a country with an army, but an army with a country. Its economy is a shambles, with record inflation and unemployment. Its pro-democracy and human rights activists have suffered another setback. But Egypt remains an ally of the West, continuing cooperation in counter-terrorism and regional security campaigns.

The one success story of the Arab Spring, tenuous though it is, is Tunisia, where the Arab Spring began. Tunisia came under French control in the nineteenth century and gained independence only in 1956. As it struggled to overcome 75 years of foreign exploitation, its wealth increasingly concentrated among secular elites who were suspicious of religion. As happened in Turkey and Iran, the government limited the role of religion, secularizing education and laws. Social discontent was exacerbated by economic troubles in the late 1970s, resulting in labor strikes and public demonstrations against the president. These were brutally suppressed.

In this context, reformist political movements developed. Tunisia is 98% Muslim, so naturally some of the reform movements used Islamic terms of reference. The one that became most popular was the progressive Islamic Tendency Movement

(*Mouvement de la Tendance Islamique*, MTI), which focused on Islamic values of human equality and social justice. These values were expressed as demands for greater economic and political participation: a living wage and true democracy. But Tunisia's elitist government began to feel threatened by MTI's growing popularity.

More economic woes in the 1980s led to more demonstrations. MTI leaders were arrested and sentenced to harsh prison terms. In 1987, Tunisia's President Habib Bourguiba was replaced by Zine El Abidine Ben Ali, who reversed some of the country's anti-religious legislation, and expanded political freedoms.

Ben Ali also tried to ban MTI. They changed their name to the Renaissance Party – al-Nahda – and some ran as independents, and won. Ben Ali and other militant secularists intensified their campaign against al-Nahda, which led to radicalization among some Islamists. Al-Nahda maintained its staunchly non-violent approach but it was nonetheless blamed for terrorist attacks. Thousands were arrested; many died in custody, and others were sentenced to long prison terms. Fear swept the country. Many activists went into exile; the United Kingdom granted al-Nahda leader Rached Ghannouchi political asylum in 1993. Repression continued throughout the 1990s, and unemployment soared.

That was the background for the spark that ignited the flame of populist uprisings that swept the Middle East and came to be called the Arab Spring. In December 2010, Mohamed Bouazizi, a 26-year-old trying to support his mother and siblings by selling fruit on the street, was slapped by a policewoman for not having a license and rebuffed by the government when he sought assistance. He couldn't take it anymore. He went back to the street, doused himself with gasoline, and set himself on fire. The news of this tragic event went viral. Across the country, people filled the streets to protest the decades of repression and unfair treatment of the poor. Brutal efforts by the government to suppress the unrest only spurred them on. Within a month, Ben Ali had resigned and went into exile in Saudi Arabia.

Exiled leaders returned to Tunisia, and elections were held for members of a constituent assembly to draft a new constitution. Like its counterpart the Muslim Brotherhood in Egypt, the Islamist al-Nahda Party was the best organized and its calls for economic reform and human rights were the most widely known. Al-Nahda therefore readily dominated the elections. It worked with secular parties, but the instability of revolution was exploited by jihadis. Two staunch secularist leaders were assassinated, and tensions mounted as the economy stalled. Popular discontent exploded in mass demonstrations during the summer of 2013. The secular Nidaa Tounes party won the 2014 elections, and Islamists and leftists continue to serve with the ruling coalition. Their collaborative work was recognized in 2015 when the Nobel Committee awarded the Peace Prize to the Tunisian National Dialogue Quartet – comprising Tunisia's General Labor Union, its Confederation of Industry, Trade, and Handicrafts, its Human Rights League, and its National Order of Lawyers.

These country profiles are examples of how *most* Muslims go about trying to address the challenges of post-colonial recovery and development. Within these countries are any number of other individuals and organizations contributing to that struggle, such as charities fighting to bring healthcare, education, and disaster relief around the world. Many have been recognized internationally. In 2006, the Nobel Peace Prize went to Bangladeshi economist Muhammad Yunus, founder of the Grameen Bank, which developed "micro finance" as a vehicle for poverty reduction. Three Muslim women have also won the Nobel Peace Prize: Iranian human rights lawyer Shireen Ebadi (2003), Yemeni Islamist human rights activist Karman Tawakkol (2011), and Pakistan's Malala Yousafzai (2014), who, along with India's Kailash Satyarthi, won the Prize for promoting children's rights. Egyptian writer Naguib Mahfouz was honored with the Nobel Prize for Literature in 1988, as was Turkish writer Orhan Pamuk in 2006. Pakistan's Mohammad Abdul Salam shared the 1979 Nobel Prize for Physics with American Steven Weinberg. Egyptian-American Ahmed Zewali received the 1999 Nobel Prize for Chemistry, and Turkey's Aziz Sancar won the same Prize in 2015. These and many others are respected among mainstream Muslims as representing their values by contributing to the global community. It is this, and not the global jihadis' terrorist campaign against the West, that characterizes their achievements.

6

Religion Is Not the Root of Conflict

In a 1989 interview with US journalist John Miller, Osama bin Laden predicted "a black future for America." The country would be fragmented and it would "have to carry the bodies of its sons back" home.[1] In a May 2015 speech, Islamic State leader Abu Bakr al-Baghdadi begged God to "deal with America and its allies," to "obliterate their wealth," and "give us victory over the disbelieving people."[2] As discussed in the preceding chapters, for many in the West, chilling statements like these were their first introduction to Muslims. It's not surprising that they have led to generalizations about all Muslims – and about Islam itself – being anti-West.

Characterizations of Islam as the basis of some Muslims' hostility to Western governments actually started long before the rise of contemporary terrorism. In 1897, as a young officer in the British cavalry stationed in India, Winston Churchill witnessed warriors resisting Britain's efforts to expand from its bases in northern India into the mountainous Afghan regions of the subcontinent's northwest. He attributed the ferocity of their resistance not to the natural inclination toward self-defense or even to the warriors' personal bravery. Instead, it was their religion giving them "incentives to slaughter" and compelling them to fight with "a wild and merciless fanaticism."[3] The following year, describing Sudanis resisting British colonizing efforts, Churchill seemed genuinely surprised that they didn't recognize the benefits the British would bring. Again, he attributed their resistance to Islam. "No stronger retrograde force exists in the world," he concluded.[4]

In today's world, stereotypes like these have morphed into political theory. Beyond mere xenophobes and Islamophobes, there are serious scholars who are convinced that Islam, the religion, is on a collision course with the West. The hypothesis proposing this inevitable "clash of civilizations" developed in the late twentieth century. After two brutal global wars in the first half of the century, the second half was dominated by the Cold War between the capitalist "West" and the Communist "East." The Cold War was in reality quite hot for more than a quarter of the century, as the West battled the East in Korea, Vietnam, Afghanistan, and elsewhere, with devastating social and economic consequences. But by the 1990s, the Cold War had ended. The Soviet Union collapsed and "the East" ceased to be Communist. Many of its former satellite states achieved independence and developed democratic governments. This gave rise among some theoreticians to optimism about the future of democracy. Now that the dark shadow of Communist totalitarianism had passed, all societies could progress toward the liberal democratic models established by "the West." That prediction was made by American political scientist Francis Fukuyama in his highly influential *The End of History and the Last Man*.[5]

But Fukuyama's former teacher, political scientist Samuel Huntington, disagreed. He argued that neither countries dominated by Marxist-Leninist governments nor those dominated by non-Western Christian religions were likely to develop democracy. The dominant religion in "the West," Christianity, is compatible with democracy, Huntington argued, but that is not the case with other religions. The democracy-incompatible religions included even Eastern Christianity. But Huntington's main target was Islam, with Confucianism as a close runner-up for those societies least likely to democratize. In Huntington's view, there was no cause for Fukuyama-esque optimism about a future of global democratic harmony. People have always been at each other's throats, he claimed. In ancient times, we were divided into competing tribes, then into competing empires, then into competing states, and then into competing ideological blocs. The one constant in human history is conflict; the post-Cold War era will be no different, argued Huntington. In two landmark publications in the 1990s, he famously predicted the coming of a "clash of civilizations."[6] This he saw as replacing the struggle between the US and Soviet superpowers, such that if there were to be a new "world war," this would be "a war between civilizations."[7] In particular, the conflict would be between "Western civilization" and what Huntington characterized as a distinctive, unitary Islamic civilization.

The "clash" hypothesis caused an uproar, of course. Huntington based his arguments on, *inter alia*, vague generalizations about Europe's tradition of separating religion and politics, and Muslims' lack of familiarity with classical Greek heritage. He overlooked the fact that a significant part of European history involved struggles between religious and secular authorities. And he was apparently unaware that classical Islamic political theory actually separates executive and legislative duties, reserving the latter for properly trained scholars supported by institutions independent of the government. He was also unfamiliar with the fact that Western Europe discovered its classical heritage when the Greek masterworks were translated into Arabic and then into Europe's language of learning, Latin. Besides its shoddy scholarship, Huntington's hypothesis reflects a mash-up of the European modernist tendency to distrust religion, and residual suspicion of Islam in particular, the religion of Europe's erstwhile competitors. European v. Ottoman competition, as well as Muslims' resistance to Europe's colonial ventures, cast long shadows over Europe. As Huntington put it in 1993, Islam has a "bloody" heritage. In 1996, he intensified the claim: "No single statement in my [1993] *Foreign Affairs* article attracted more critical comment than: 'Islam has bloody borders.' I made that judgment on the basis of a casual survey of intercivilizational conflicts. Quantitative evidence from every disinterested source conclusively demonstrates its validity."[8]

Huntington's hypothesis is named for a phrase that was actually coined by a scholar who shares the perception that Islam and the West are inevitably in conflict. Bernard Lewis, a renowned historian of the Middle East, argues that "Islam" resents the powerful non-Muslim West, and has done so since the Ottomans failed to conquer Vienna in 1683.[9] Lewis claims further that it is very natural that Muslims should hate the West. Why? Because of its geopolitical dominance. Until Europeans took control of most Muslim-majority regions during the eighteenth and nineteenth centuries, Muslims were generally governed by Muslims and controlled their own destinies. But that all stopped with the rise of modern European states. They turned the tables, resisting Ottoman expansion, colonizing Muslim lands, and ultimately dismantling mighty medieval Muslim empires. So unlike Huntington, for whom religion is the problem, for Lewis, geopolitical competition is the core of the struggle. But in both scholars' perspectives, the West and the Muslim world have been and will remain archenemies. And their views are highly influential. Lewis was an informal White House advisor during the administration of George W. Bush, and is widely credited with inspiring the US-led invasion of Iraq in 2003.[10] As journalist Peter Waldman wrote in a 2004 *Wall Street Journal* article, Lewis "helped coax the White House" into framing the problem of terrorism post-9/11 as a problem with Islam.[11]

Whether or not Huntington and Lewis actually bear responsibility for framing the political struggles between Euro-America and Muslim-majority countries in religious terms, their claim that "the West" and "Islam" are locked in bloody competition is widely known among Muslims. And given Muslims' residual resentment of colonialism, and the literally incalculable destruction of life and property resulting from "the West's" ongoing wars in Afghanistan and Iraq, the "clash" hypothesis unquestionably epitomizes for many Muslims a distinct antipathy toward Islam. The 2007 World Public Opinion survey cited in Chapter 3, for example, which was conducted in Morocco, Egypt, Pakistan, and Indonesia, indicates that "large majorities believe that undermining Islam is a key goal of US foreign policy." The report quotes World Public Opinion editor Steven Kull summarizing: "While US leaders may frame the conflict as a war on terrorism, people in the Islamic world clearly perceive the US as being at war with Islam."[12] The Gallup poll cited in Chapters 1 and 3, the most extensive poll ever taken of Muslim public opinion worldwide, showed that the majority of Muslims believe the Western-led Global War on Terrorism (GWOT, in military terms) is predicated on disrespect for their religion – or, more precisely, on the conflation of Islam and terrorism.[13]

That perception helps explain the terrorists' religiously framed denunciations of the West, and this is why some scholars today insist that, in fact, Islam is at the root of terrorism. Journalist Graeme Wood set off a raucous debate when he quoted Princeton scholar Bernard Haykel countering the claims of mainstream Muslim organizations that the terrorists were "un-Islamic." Haykel dismissed mainstream denunciations of terrorism as "politically correct," "cotton-candy" views that are "sustainable only through willful ignorance." In fact, says Haykel, Islamic State warriors are "deeply infused with religious vigor."[14]

There is no doubt that Haykel is right. As the name "Islamic State" makes clear, that group and many others use Islamic terms of reference in their campaigns against Western policies. But his conclusion that "these guys have just as much legitimacy as anyone else" does not follow. Their language is Islamic, but does that make their interpretations "legitimate"? Not if the criteria for legitimacy include the positions of qualified religious authorities worldwide or Muslim opinion overall. Haykel points out that atrocities (he names slavery, crucifixion, and beheadings) were actually practiced by Muslim warriors in the distant past as they expanded their power base from Arabia throughout the Middle East, across North Africa, and into Asia. That is also probably true, as New York University historian Robert Hoyland points out. He says that "[t]he Arab empire," like all empires, used a combination of violence and non-violent strategies to establish and maintain control.[15] But it is also true that, like other religions, Islam has evolved significantly since the seventh century. Over the intervening centuries, Muslim authorities have developed the positions expressed in the overwhelming condemnation of terrorist atrocities that we have discussed. Indeed, Wood acknowledges that "nearly all" Muslims reject IS as representative of Islam.

The political roots of conflict

So while the majority of Muslims struggle peacefully for good governance and economic development within their communities, a small minority call for global jihad against the mighty West. That minority are represented by al-Qaeda and its offshoot Islamic State. Al-Qaeda focuses on fighting the West; IS adds to that agenda the claiming of territory and governance under its retrograde version of Islamic law. Taking advantage of situations in which government has broken down and the chaos prevailing in war zones, IS seeks to coopt regional terrorist groups like Nigeria's Boko Haram and Somalia's al-Shabaab. But both al-Qaeda and IS are inspired by veteran jihadi strategist Abu Bakr al-Naji's *The Management of Savagery* (see Chapter 2). That book lays out detailed plans to lure Muslims away from mainstream Islamic positions. Al-Naji ridicules those who accept mainstream Islamic views as ignorant "propagandists" and condemns their efforts to forge bonds with non-Muslims and secularists in order to fight the jihadis. Instead, he directs his lieutenants to exploit differences among people. They must continue to berate the mainstream Muslims as cowards and traitors for cooperating with the West. The global jihadis must "transform societies into two opposing groups." They have to launch terror attacks that cause so much chaos that people will welcome them when they come in and impose their brand of order. The war must be total; people will have to choose between global jihadis and the West. And it won't matter how many Muslims die in the process.[16]

Al-Naji also strategizes for defeating the West militarily, by luring the West into wars he believes will exhaust and ultimately destroy it, just as the jihadis believe they destroyed the Soviet Union in

Afghanistan. The 9/11 attacks were designed to achieve that goal. By the time of Bin Laden's 2001 "Letter to America," the United States had indeed invaded Afghanistan. Bin Laden's 2002 message then excoriated the US for its "war crimes" in Afghanistan. He says "densely populated innocent civilian villages were destroyed, bombs were dropped on mosques … [and] Allah alone know how many people have died by torture at the hands of you and your agents." But Bin Laden's tears were of the crocodile variety. Drawing the United States into Afghanistan advanced the jihadis' efforts to convince people of the West's depravity, and at the same time position the West for effective Mao-esque guerrilla attacks.

Besides Chairman Mao, al-Naji calls on the authority of British historian Paul Kennedy. Without citing the source, al-Naji misquotes Kennedy, but he gets the point right. Kennedy wrote in his widely read 1989 *The Rise and Fall of the Great Powers* that if a country "over-extends itself geographically and strategically; if … it chooses to devote a large proportion of its total income to 'protection,' leaving less for 'productive investment,'" its economy will suffer, as will its "international standing."[17] Al-Naji's version has Kennedy claiming that America's strategic overreach will lead to its downfall. Triggering that overreach is the strategic reason for terrorist attacks. Once the West gets its "boots on the ground," the jihadis believe they will be able to exhaust and ultimately defeat it. Their language may be religious, but their goals are political and their strategies are strictly secular.

Yet even though, as Haykel put it, nearly all Muslims reject global jihadism, there remains a significant overlap between the political grievances of terrorists and those of mainstream Muslims who reject terrorism as a means of addressing them. This was recognized in a 2004 report commissioned by then US Secretary of Defense Paul Wolfowitz. The report concludes that "Muslims do not 'hate our freedom,' but rather, they hate our policies." It cites the same issues identified in both mainstream opinion polls and jihadi manifestos, including Western support for authoritarian governments that violate the human, political, and civil rights of their citizens. It also cites the devastating effects of the wars in Afghanistan and Iraq on both the citizens of those countries and the reputation of the United States. The "dramatic narrative since 9/11," whereby the West has claimed to be a liberating force despite the ongoing devastation wrought, has lent credibility to jihadi claims that it is a force for evil and must be fought. "Not only has there been a proliferation of 'terrorist' groups," the report claims, but "the unifying context of a shared cause creates a sense of affiliation across the many cultural and sectarian boundaries that divide Islam."[18]

The way forward

The complexity of the ongoing wars in the Middle East can seem mind-boggling. For example, in Iraq, the Western allies and Iran are both fighting radical Sunni terrorists in support of a Shia-dominated government. Next door in Syria, they fight on opposite sides: Iran supports the Shia government while the Western allies and the radical Sunni terrorists fight against it – and against each other. And in Yemen, Iran supports a Shia rebel group also targeted by radical Sunni terrorists, and by Saudi Arabia, with US and UK support. In addition, these conflicts overlay residual post-colonial problems in the region, such as the continued statelessness of Palestinians and Kurds. (Kurds are a predominantly Muslim ethnic minority who have sought autonomy since the nineteenth century. Following World War I, their lands were divided by foreign-imposed boundaries; the majority live in Turkey, but a large minority live in Iraq, and smaller minorities live in Syria and Iran.)

But two key points must be borne in mind. First, our perplexity pales next to the wars' savagery and the suffering they cause. The brutality of the Western-supported Saudi attacks against the Shia in Yemen – including targeting hospitals and schools – has generated allegations of war crimes.[19] It's that suffering that causes anti-West attitudes. And, second, the continuation of wars in Muslim-majority regions not only gives greater credibility to jihadi narratives but gives jihadis greater "opportunity spaces" – regions of chaos in which their recruiting and guerrilla tactics are most effective.[20]

So what is to be done? Some believe that the West must more clearly communicate its objectives so that Muslims recognize their good intentions. But the Wolfowitz-commissioned report cited above concludes that as a result of unpopular policies, American diplomacy has a "fundamental problem of credibility. Simply, there is none." The same report, with surprising clarity, recognizes that foreign intervention in Muslim-majority countries – whether direct military intervention or support for unpopular governments – has spurred the growth of terrorism. So if the goal is to continue policies as they stand – support for governments that benefit Western economic interests regardless of their domestic implications – then all the money poured into media and public relations firms to clothe old policies in new "messaging" will be wasted. Likewise, the imposition of ever-greater security measures. As recent attacks in Brussels, Istanbul, Ankara, and Lahore demonstrate, there will always be "soft targets." And as long as Western policies enable injustice, there will be people willing to attack. If, on the other hand, the goal is to counter terrorism, then the way forward is clear: address the policies that so aggravate the populations subjected to them. As award-winning French economist Thomas Piketty put it, yes, terrorist organizations must be fought. But we must also consider the political conditions, "the humiliation and the injustices" that give rise to terrorist organizations. "The real issue is the establishment of an equitable model for social development both there and here."[21]

In September 2015, I met with exiled leaders of Egypt's Muslim Brotherhood, who are currently being characterized by ruling elites as desperate terrorists. I asked them the question posed in the title of this book. Their response: "Is political self-determination an enemy of the West? Is economic autonomy an enemy of the West? Are religious freedom, freedom of expression, and freedom of association enemies of the West?" Those are the goals sought by mainstream Muslims, whether Islamist or not, so the answer to the question seems obvious. Muslims who suffer because of Western policies can become enemies of the West. But it is not because of their religion. As venerable statesman Prince Hassan of Jordan declared before the UN General Assembly in 2008, "It would seem to me obvious that we must frame the meaning of security within an expanded context … ."[22] That context: joining with global partners to address not just corporate profit but basic human rights, including access to food, healthcare, education, and political participation. These, said His Royal Highness, provide the basis for human security. And this human security is essential if we are to ensure that neither global terrorists nor Islamophobic parties can exploit political grievances to foment fear, mistrust, and hatred between Muslim and non-Muslim communities worldwide.

Further Reading

Readers interested in deepening their background on the apparent confrontation of Islam and the West (Chapter 1, "Islam v. the West?") will benefit from Bernard Lewis's "The Roots of Muslim Rage" (*The Atlantic Monthly*, September 1990: 47–60) and Samuel Huntington's classic *The Clash of Civilizations and the Remaking of World Order* (New York: Simon & Schuster, 1996). Lewis argued that Muslims would lash out against Western powers in an effort to restore finally a balance of power, lost with the demise of the Mughal and Ottoman empires. Huntington argues that Muslims' political values are inherently antithetical to those held in the West, so that confrontation between the West's liberal democratic states and Islam's authoritarian ones is inevitable. Tariq Ramadan provides a Muslim perspective on the issue in *Islam, the*

West and the Challenges of Modernity (Markfield, Leicester: The Islamic Foundation, 2009). Edward E. Curtis IV's *Bloomsbury Reader on Islam in the West* (London: Bloomsbury Academic, 2015) allows readers access to a wide range of readings documenting the long and often integrated history of Muslims and the West.

Many scholars have explored the rise and nature of global jihadism (Chapter 2, "Jihad: Message, Motivation, and Methods"). Readers seeking deeper background into its development and spread will find it in Montasser al-Zayyat's *The Road to Al-Qaeda: The Story of Bin Laden's Right-Hand Man* (London: Pluto Press, 2004). It tells the story of the current al-Qaeda leader Ayman Zawahiri's evolution from mainstream Islamist to nationalist jihadist in Egypt, to global jihadist in Afghanistan. It is particularly effective in explaining the innovation in legal theory of preemptive war against the "far enemy." Further documentation of al-Qaeda positions will be found in Gilles Keppel's *Al-Qaeda in Its Own Words* (Cambridge, MA: Belknap Press, 2010). Patrick Cockburn's *The Rise of Islamic State: ISIS and the New Sunni Revolution* (London: Verso, 2015) describes how the failure of the Western campaign in Iraq allowed the rise of Islamic State. Michael W.S. Ryan's *Decoding Al-Qaeda's*

Strategy: The Deep Battle against America (New York: Columbia University Press, 2013) is essential reading for those interested in global jihadis' guerrilla warfare strategies. *The ISIS Apocalypse: The History, Strategy, and Doomsday Vision of the Islamic State* by William McCants (New York: St Martin's Press, 2015) helps explain how Islamic State (ISIS) emerged from and broke with al-Qaeda through greater brutality and the claiming of territory. McCants also describes Islamic State's involvement with Boko Haram and al-Shabaab. Jessica Stern and J.M. Berger describe IS recruiting methods in the West, including their unique religious interpretations and "snuff videos," in *ISIS: The State of Terror* (New York: HarperCollins, 2015). Daniel Byman's *Al Qaeda, the Islamic State, and the Global Jihadist Movement: What Everyone Needs to Know* (Oxford: Oxford University Press, 2015) explains key differences between al-Qaeda and its offspring Islamic State. Those interested in the difference between global terrorist organizations (al-Qaeda and IS) and nationalist groups that use terrorist tactics (such as Palestine's Hamas and Lebanon's Hezbollah) may consult Sara Roy's *Hamas and Civil Society in Gaza: Engaging the Islamist Social Sector* (Princeton, NJ: Princeton University Press, 2013) and Augustus Richard

Norton's *Hezbollah: A Short History* (Princeton, NJ: Princeton University Press, 2014).

Mainstream Muslim opposition to terrorism is well documented (Chapter 3, "Muslim Opposition to Terror"). John L. Esposito and Dalia Mogahed's *Who Speaks for Islam? What a Billion Muslims Really Think* (New York: Gallup Press, 2007), based on the first global sampling of Muslim public opinion, demonstrates that Muslims overwhelmingly reject terrorism, and seek democratic governance, human rights, and development. The classic work on Islamic rules of warfare is Majid Khadduri's *War and Peace in the Law of Islam* (Clark, NJ: The Lawbook Exchange, 2015; originally published in 1955). Reuven Firestone's *Jihad: The Origin of Holy War in Islam* (Oxford: Oxford University Press, 2002) and *Holy War in Judaism: The Rise and Fall of a Controversial Idea* (Oxford: Oxford University Press, 2012) provide an interesting contrast to classical theories. John L. Esposito's *Unholy War: Terror in the Name of Islam* (Oxford: Oxford University Press, 2003) is a good source for understanding the rise of terrorism and the unique uses of Islamic terms of reference made by terrorists. Ghazi bin Muhammad and Ibrahim Kalin's *War and Peace in Islam: The Uses and Abuses of Jihad* (Great Shelford, Cambridge: Islamic Texts Society,

2013) brings together diverse scholars' careful refutations of terrorist arguments about the permissibility of violence. Seyyed Hossein Nasr's *Islam in the Modern World: Challenged by the West, Threatened by Fundamentalism, Keeping Faith with Tradition* (New York: HarperOne, 2012) presents the deeply spiritual perspective of traditional Islam in its opposition to both the materialism of secular modernity and the distinctly non-traditional violence of Islamic extremism. Karen Armstrong's *Fields of Blood: Religion and the History of Violence* (New York: Anchor, 2015) allows readers to place Islamic terrorism within a broader historical context. Arguing against those who claim religion is the source of violence, Armstrong claims that it nevertheless is readily available to rationalize political objectives.

Readers seeking greater background into specific areas of concern to Muslims worldwide (Chapter 4, "Shared Grievances") will find the following helpful: James Gelvin, *The Israel–Palestine Conflict: One Hundred Years of War* (Cambridge: Cambridge University Press, 2016); Rashid Khalidi, *The Iron Cage: The Story of the Palestinian Struggle for Statehood* (New York: Beacon, 2007); Anna Politkovskaya and Alexander Burry, *A Small Corner of Hell: Dispatches from*

Chechnya (Chicago: University of Chicago Press, 2003); Sumantra Bose, *Kashmir: Roots of Conflict, Paths to Peace* (Cambridge, MA: Harvard University Press, 2005); and Azeem Ibrahim, *The Rohingyas: Inside Myanmar's Hidden Genocide* (London: Hurst, 2016).

Muslim countries' ongoing struggles for democratization (Chapter 5, "Mainstream Muslim Strategies") have been the subject of numerous scholarly works, particularly in light of the Arab Spring uprisings in 2010–11. James Gelvin's *The Arab Uprisings: What Everyone Needs to Know* (Oxford: Oxford University Press, 2015) provides a useful overview. John L. Esposito, John O. Voll, and Tamara Sonn's *Islam and Democracy after the Arab Spring* (Oxford: Oxford University Press, 2015) traces the trajectories in Iran, Pakistan, Indonesia, Senegal, Tunisia, and Egypt. Its references direct readers to sources for deeper background on theories, trends, and specific examples of democratization in Muslim-majority countries.

Gilles Kepel's *The War for Muslim Minds: Islam and the West* (Cambridge, MA: Belknap Press, 2006) is recommended for those interested in further background to Chapter 6 ("Religion Is Not the Root of Conflict"). It provides an insightful analysis of the impact of the Global War on Terror, arguing that the West's military activities have been disastrous for Muslim civil society, undermined efforts at political reform and economic development, and, in the process, provided new recruits for international terrorist organizations. Tariq Ramadan's *Islamic Ethics: A Very Short Introduction* (Oxford: Oxford University Press, 2014) gives a brief, clear description of mainstream Muslim values. Raymond William Baker's *Islam without Fear: Egypt and the New Islamists* (Cambridge, MA: Harvard University Press, 2006) will help readers understand the objectives of mainstream Islamists such as the Muslim Brotherhood.

Notes

Chapter 1 Islam v. the West?

1 Daesh (*da`ish*) is an acronym for the group's original name, Islamic State in Iraq and Syria (*al-dawlat al-islamiyyah fi'l-`iraq wa'l-sham)*. Similar to another Arabic term (*da`s*) meaning, roughly, "to trample or crush," it is a derogatory term used by the group's opponents – that is, most of the world. ISIL and ISIS are the English initials for variant translations of *al-sham*: the Levant (an archaic term for the eastern Mediterranean) and Syria.

2 "Full Text: Bin Laden's 'Letter to America'," *The Guardian*, November 24, 2002 (http://www.theguardian.com/world/2002/nov/24/theobserver).

3 Glenn Beck, *It IS About Islam: Exposing the Truth about ISIS, Al Qaeda, Iran, and the Caliphate* (New York: Threshold Editions/Mercury Radio Arts, 2015), p. 8.

4 See John L. Esposito and Dalia Mogahed, *Who Speaks for Islam? What a Billion Muslims Really*

Think (New York: Gallup Press, 2007), pp. 69–70, 74, 77.

5 Michael Lipka, "Muslims and Islam: Key Findings in the US and around the World," Pew Research Center, December 7, 2015 (http://www.pewresearch.org/fact-tank/2015/12/07/muslims-and-islam-key-findings-in-the-u-s-and-around-the-world/).

6 http://kurzman.unc.edu/Islamic-statements-against-terrorism/.

Chapter 2 Jihad: Message, Motivation, and Methods

1 "Bin Laden's Fatwa," August 23, 1996 (http://www.pbs.org/newshour/updates/military-july-dec96-fatwa_1996/).

2 Published in Arabic in *al-Quds al-Arabi*, London, February 23, 1998, p. 3 (https://www.library.cornell.edu/colldev/mideast/fatw2.htm); translation by FAS (http://fas.org/irp/world/para/docs/980223-fatwa.htm).

3 "Full Text: Bin Laden's 'Letter to America'," *The Guardian*, November 24, 2002 (http://www.theguardian.com/world/2002/nov/24/theobserver).

4 "What Did Abu Bakr al-Baghdadi Say?" *Middle East Eye*, July 5, 2014 (http://www.middleeasteye.net/news/what-did-baghdad-say-320749010).

5 "In New Audio Speech, Islamic State ISIS Leader Al-Baghdadi Issues Call to Arms to All Muslims," The Middle East Media Research Institute, May

14, 2015 (http://www.memrijttm.org/in-new-audio-speech-islamic-state-isis-leader-al-baghdadi-issues-call-to-arms-to-all-muslims.html).

6 Institute for Economics and Peace, *Global Terrorism Index 2015* (http://static.visionofhumanity.org/sites/default/files/2015%20Global%20Terrorism%20Index%20Report_0_0.pdf).

7 National Counterterrorism Center, "2011 Report on Terrorism" (Washington DC: Office of the Director of National Intelligence, 2012), p. 14.

8 "Concerns about Islamic Extremism on the Rise in the Middle East," Pew Research Center, July 1, 2014 (http://www.pewglobal.org/2014/07/01/concerns-about-islamic-extremism-on-the-rise-in-middle-east/).

9 M. Cherif Bassiouni, "Misunderstanding Islam on the Use of Violence," *Houston Journal of International Law*. 37:3 (July 2015): 645–6.

10 Abu Bakr al-Naji, *Idarat al-Tawahhush* (Management of Savagery). English translation: *The Management of Savagery: The Most Critical Stage Through Which the Umma Will Pass*, trans. William McCants (Cambridge, MA: The John M. Olin Institute for Strategic Studies, 2006), pp. 21–2 (https://azelin.files.wordpress.com/2010/08/abu-bakr-naji-the-management-of-savagery-the-most-critical-stage-through-which-the-umma-will-pass.pdf).

11 Abu Mus`ab al-Suri, *Da`wat al-Muqawamat al-Islamiyyat al-`Alamiyyah* (The Call to Global Islamic Resistance) (https://archive.org/details/Dawaaah). Partial translation: *The Global Islamic Resis-*

tance Call (https://archive.org/stream/TheGlobal IslamicResistanceCall/The_Global_Islamic_Resis tance_Call_Chapter_8_sections_5_to_7_LIST_OF_ TARGETS#page/n0/mode/1up), Chapter 8, Section 6.

12 Abu Amru al-Qa`idi, "A Course in the Art of Recruiting," *Onemagazine* (http://www.onemaga zine.es/pdf/al-qaeda-manual.pdf).

13 "Translation of 'Revolutionary Wars'," in Michael W.S. Ryan, *Decoding Al-Qaeda's Strategy: The Deep Battle against America* (New York: Columbia University Press, 2013), pp. 271–2.

14 "Bin Laden's Fatwa" (as note 1).

Chapter 3 Muslim Opposition to Terror

1 Michael W.S. Ryan, *Decoding Al-Qaeda's Strategy: The Deep Battle against America* (New York: Columbia University Press, 2013), p. 60.

2 "Muslim Public Opinion on US Policy, Attacks on Civilians and al Qaeda," World Public Opinion.org., April 24, 2007 (http://www.worldpublicopinion.org/pipa/pdf/apr07/START_Apr07_rpt.pdf).

3 John L. Esposito and Dalia Mogahed, *Who Speaks for Islam? What a Billion Muslims Really Think* (New York: Gallup Press, 2007), pp. 69–70.

4 Gallup World Poll, "Views of Violence" (http://www.gallup.com/poll/157067/views-violence.aspx?g_source=MUSLIM_STUDIES&g_medium=topic&g_campaign=tiles).

5 The statements just cited and others have been

compiled and are available at kurzman.unc.edu/Islamic-statements-against-terrorism/, for example.

6 "Open Letter to Al-Baghdadi" (http:// www.lettertobaghdadi.com/).

7 M. Cherif Bassiouni, "Misunderstanding Islam on the Use of Violence," *Houston Journal of International Law*, 37:3 (July 2015): 651.

8 http://www.kurzman.unc.edu/Islamic-statements-against-terrorism/. Interview, December 16–18, 2005, London–Leeds–Manchester.

Chapter 4 Shared Grievances

1 "Text: President Bush Addresses the Nation," September 20, 2001 (http://www.washingtonpost.com/wp-srv/nation/specials/attacked/transcripts/bushaddress_092001.html).

2 "Full Text: Bin Laden's 'Letter to America'," *The Guardian*, November 24, 2002 (http://www.theguardian.com/world/2002/nov/24/theobserver).

3 http://kurzman.unc.edu/Islamic-statements-against-terrorism/; Islamic Republic News Agency, September 16, 2001.

4 John Powers, *Sore Winners: American Idols, Patriotic Shoppers, and Other Strange Species in George Bush's America* (New York: Anchor, 2005), p. 95. As if to confirm that point, Public Policy Polling released results of US public opinion in December 2015, indicating that of 532 Republicans asked if they would support the bombing of Agrabah, nearly a third said they would; just over half said they

weren't sure. Agrabah is the fictional kingdom in the Disney cartoon *Aladdin.* Jana Kasperkevic, "Poll: 30% of GOP Voters Support Bombing Agrabah, the City from Aladdin," *The Guardian*, December 18, 2015 (http://www.theguardian.com/us-news/2015/dec/18/republican-voters-bomb-agrabah-disney-aladdin-donald-trump).

5 "Palestinian Refugee Numbers/Whereabouts," IRIN, June 22, 2010 (http://www.irinnews.org/report/89571/middle-east-palestinian-refugee-numbers-whereabouts); https://www.unrwausa.org/.

6 "Israel and Occupied Palestinian Territories 2015/2016," Amnesty International Annual Report 2015/2016 (https://www.amnesty.org/en/countries/middle-east-and-north-africa/israel-and-occupied-palestinian-territories/report-israel-and-occupied-palestinian-territories/).

7 Boutros Boutros-Ghali, *Unvanquished: A US–UN Saga* (New York: Random House, 1999), p. 138. For information on the related conflict in Ethiopia's Ogaden region, see Ogaden Human Rights Committee, "Human Rights Violations in the Ogaden by the Ethiopian Government, 1991 to 1996," July 1996 (http://www.ogadenrights.org/Human_Rights_Violations.pdf).

8 Human Rights Watch, "World Report 2015: Burma (Events of 2014)" (https://www.hrw.org/world-report/2015/country-chapters/burma).

9 Samar Batrawi, "Understanding ISIS's Palestine Propaganda," Al-Shabaka: The Palestinian Policy Network, March 31, 2016 (https://al-shabaka.org/

commentaries/understanding-isiss-palestine-propaganda/).

Chapter 5 Mainstream Muslim Strategies

1 See, for example, Fergus Hanson, "Indonesia Poll 2012: Shattering Stereotypes: Public Opinion and Foreign Policy," Lowy Institute for International Policy (http://www.lowyinstitute.org/files/lowy_indonesia_poll_2012.pdf).
2 United Nations Development Programme, "Table 1: Human Development Index and Its Components" (hdr.undp.org/composite/HDI).

Chapter 6 Religion Is Not the Root of Conflict

1 Interview with Osama bin Laden, Frontline, Pbs.org, May 1998 (http://www.pbs.org/wgbh/pages/frontline/shows/binladen/who/interview.html).
2 "In New Audio Speech, Islamic State ISIS Leader Al-Baghdadi Issues Call to Arms to All Muslims," The Middle East Media Research Institute, May 14, 2015 (http://www.memrijttm.org/in-new-audio-speech-islamic-state-isis-leader-al-baghdadi-issues-call-to-arms-to-all-muslims.html).
3 Winston Churchill, *The Story of the Malakand Field Force: An Episode of Frontier War* (New York: Dover, 2010 [1898]), p. 4.
4 Winston Churchill, *The River War* (London: Longmans, Green & Company, 1899), 1st edn, Vol. II, p. 248.

5 Francis Fukuyama, *The End of History and the Last Man* (New York: Free Press 1993).
6 Samuel P. Huntington, "The Clash of Civilizations?," *Foreign Affairs*, Summer 1993: 22–49; *The Clash of Civilizations and the Remaking of World Order* (New York: Simon & Schuster, 1996).
7 Huntington, "The Clash of Civilizations?," p. 39.
8 Huntington, *The Clash of Civilizations*, p. 258.
9 Bernard Lewis, "The Roots of Muslim Rage," *The Atlantic Monthly*, September 1990: 47–60.
10 Josh Nathan-Kazis, "Neocons Gather to Fete Iraq War Godfather Bernard Lewis," *Forward*, September 20, 2012 (http://forward.com/news/163089/neocons-gather-to-fete-iraq-war-godfather-bernard/),
11 Peter Waldman, "Containing Jihad: A Historian's Take on Islam Steers US in Terrorism Fight. Bernard Lewis's Blueprint: Sowing Arab Democracy Is Facing a Test in Iraq – The 'Clash of Civilizations'," *Wall Street Journal*, February 3, 2004 (http://www.pierretristam.com/Bobst/library/wf-214.htm).
12 "Muslims Believe US Seeks to Undermine Islam," WorldPublicOpinion.org, April 24, 2007 (http://www.worldpublicopinion.org/pipa/articles/brmiddleeastnafricara/346.php).
13 John L. Esposito and Dalia Mogahed, *Who Speaks for Islam? What a Billion Muslims Really Think* (New York: Gallup Press, 2007), pp. 86–7.
14 Graeme Wood, "What ISIS Really Wants." *The Atlantic*, March 2015. (http://www.theatlantic.com/magazine/archive/2015/03/what-isi-really-wants/384980/).

15 Robert G. Hoyland, *In God's Path: The Arab Conquests and the Creation of an Islamic Empire* (New York: Oxford University Press, 2014), p. 56.
16 Abu Bakr al-Naji, *Idarat al-Tawahhush* (Management of Savagery), p. 46 (Section 7). English translation: *The Management of Savagery: The Most Critical Stage Through Which the Umma Will Pass*, trans. William McCants (Cambridge, MA: The John M. Olin Institute for Strategic Studies, 2006), p. 108 (https://azelin.files.wordpress.com/2010/08/abu-bakr-naji-the-management-of-savagery-the-most-critical-stage-through-which-the-umma-will-pass.pdf).
17 Paul Kennedy, *The Rise and Fall of the Great Powers* (New York: Vintage, 1989), p. 539.
18 Defense Science Board, "Report of the Defense Science Board Task Force on Strategic Communication" (Washington DC: Office of the Under Secretary of Defense for Acquisition, Technology, and Logistics, September 2004) (http://fas.org/irp/agency/dod/dsb/commun.pdf), p. 40/111.
19 Colum Lynch, "US Support for Saudi Strikes in Yemen Raises War Crimes Concerns," *Foreign Policy*, October 15, 2015 (http://foreignpolicy.com/015/10/15/u-s-support-for-saudi-strikes-in-yemen-raises-war-crime-concerns/).
20 See Michael Guntner, Till Paasche, and Nahro Zagros, "Understanding ISIS," *Journal of South Asian and Middle Eastern Studies*, XXXVIII/2 (Winter 2015): 1.
21 Thomas Piketty, "Clamping Down with Law and

Order Will Not be Enough," *Le Monde*, November 24, 2015 (http://piketty.blog.lemonde.fr/2015/11/24/clamping-down-with-law-and-order-will-not-be-enough/).

22 HRH Prince El Hassan bin Talal, Thematic Debate on Human Security, United Nations General Assembly, New York, May 22, 2008, "Dignity and Justice for All of Us: Human Security on the Global Commons" (http://www.un.org/ga/president/62/statements/hrhelhasanspeech.pdf).